American, Living Large in Mexico

Part 2

Making the Move
The Real Deal

Mexico

USA

From Bill the Geek

Table of Contents

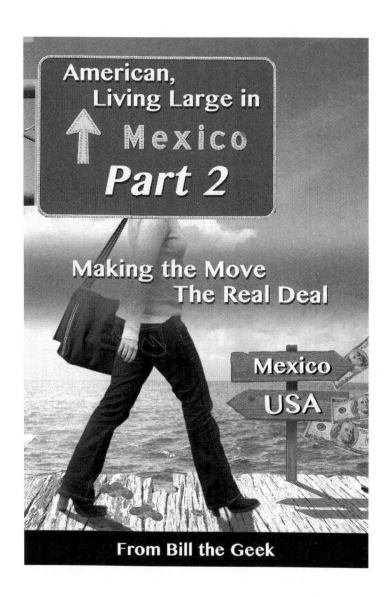

American, Living Large in **Mexico** *Part 2*

Making the Move The Real Deal

Mexico

USA

From Bill the Geek

Prelude

Hi, this is Bill the Geek, Bill Dallas Lewis, Dartmouth College, Ohio State University Grad, full fledged Geek.

This is part 2 of, "American Living Large in Mexico. Making the Move, The Real Deal."

In part 1, I went over the basics, but in this part, I get into the very specifics of making the move to Mexico and working online so that you can earn good money online from countries that pay good money. Countries like Great Britain, The United States, Australia and other English speaking countries where people will pay you online and this money will go into your USA bank account.

How this book was written.

The following text is from me talking into my computer, going from chapter idea to the next chapter idea. It was not written, the text all comes from the spoken word. After I recorded the whole thing, I had a wonderful person in Europe transcribe the voice into text.

Thus, this book is like listening to someone, me, talking. Sentences will run together and the grammar may not read like you standard, stiff written word.

Website and SEO Information.

In later chapters I will tell you how to help people find you on the internet by building a web site and writing the website with excellent SEO, Search Engine Optimization techniques that will put you on page 1 of Google.

I mean this several times in the book. To see the videos that will teach you how to build your website and how to get on page 1 of Google, simply go to my website;

http://billthegeek.com/members

or

http://sillybilly.com

There is a link at the top of sillybilly.com that will say, "Divi SEO, and Divi Video Tutorials."

Click there and then you will see the videos that I talk about later in this book.

Chapter 1 - Introduction

Welcome to *American Living Large in Mexico, Part Two*, Planning the Move to Mexico. This is *Bill the Geek* and I'll be your guide through this journey. Welcome, welcome, welcome and thanks for downloading or visiting the audio for Part two. In this introduction I'm going to touch base on a little bit of what we covered in Part one, just how I ended up in Mexico.

The accident that happened that actually got me to Mexico is a real good blueprint of what you need to prepare for to get down here and to be functioning and to be earning money and to be living comfortably in Mexico in the warmth, with all this good food, saving lots of money and living a great life and being very happy. So what happened to me was I was teaching **advanced computer graphics** out in San Francisco, California and **Citigroup** called me up and they wanted to me to teach their senior animators, *Flash*, the animation program.

So I said "okay, I can do it, but where are you located?"

They said, "Well, we're in New York City."

Well, I'm in San Francisco, they're in New York City and I asked them how are we going to do that. And they said well, we'll just use Go to Meeting. Then our designers can see your computer, we have FM quality sound, you can show them what to do, we can see everybody's computers, everybody's good to go. I said okay, fine. So what happened was is over the course of the month I would, you know, be down at the office at 4 o'clock in the morning talking to them at 7 o'clock in the morning Eastern Standard Time. And I taught them Flash. So anyway, I'd been teaching *Advanced Computer Graphics* and Web Design for five years to senior designers in San Francisco.

And after five years I had learned a lot, I was ready to make the move to something else. I wasn't quite sure what to do, so I thought I would give my hometown Columbus, Ohio a try to see if maybe I could make a living there. I had a business development, an online business development job, that I could do anywhere so I could take that with me until I decided what I was going to do next. So I got to Columbus, Ohio.

You know, Columbus, Ohio was okay. It's a white-collar town, Ohio State University, federal government, big insurance, city. There are things to do in Columbus, Ohio, but when I got there after two weeks of visiting old friends and family I started to get kind of bored. And then it hit me that, you know, Bill, you could teach Graphic courses online everywhere in the country. You just go to Meeting, you can teach Photoshop, Dreamweaver, HTML, CSS, Flash, Web Development, Search Engine Optimization. You can teach people all over the United States how to do this.

And at that time, Craigslist was good for getting into different cities and posting ads in different cities all around the United States, which you can't do anymore. But anyway, so I got on Craigslist, posted ads in every city in the United States for Web Design, this and that. And the next thing I know, people were contacting me from all over the United States to do these things and we would get on Go to Meeting, have our sessions, they would pay me via PayPal after the session and it really started kicking off. I built a website, did SEO on the website, I was picking up clients, do SEO, Search Engine Optimization to the website.

And all of the sudden I was saving a bunch of money. Through the process I was living with one of my best friends who was with a media company, the media company shut down and he was trying to find a job, a sales job. And his situation was he wanted to make anything over 100,000 dollars a year and he would do about anything to make this amount of money and I watched him go through the interview process with these strange companies that to me had nothing to do with living life. And the more I stayed in Columbus, the more it was hitting me that I don't know if I can be happy living in this city. I mean what is life, what is life all about? And then it hit me that life is about being happy. Where can you live and be happy, Bill?

And so I studied Spanish in a city called **San Luis Potosi** in Mexico when I was earning my degree at **Dartmouth College**. And I remember that people told me while I was in that program they visited *Puerto Vallarta*, Mexico, how wonderful the beaches were, how great the people were. And when I was in San Luis Potosi the Mexican community treated me great. They were inviting me to their houses for dinner, all kinds of things to do, it was warm in the winter time... So I started to think "wow", you know, I can do this business anywhere on the planet. And especially, this especially hit me when December came and it went down to 17 degrees.

Well, it gets chilly in San Francisco, but it didn't go down to 17 degrees and start snowing. I mean 17 degrees is like freezing. And in the house where I was living, I was living on the third floor, it was really cold. I was wearing like, literally I was wearing like four pairs of pants and five pairs of socks and three coats, 24/ 7. And when I took a bath or a shower it was a torture exercise. You had to take off all your clothes and freeze to death, get in the hot water and then get out of the hot water, freeze to death and I said "No, no, this is not happy."

Bill needs to live happy.

So what I did was I got on the internet. I got on the Internet and I said, you know, maybe I could live in Puerto Vallarta, Mexico, what the heck.

I'd never been there before. So the Internet is such a library of international information. I got on the Internet and I did a search for apartments. I wanted to know how much it would cost to get an apartment in Puerto Vallarta. So I did a search, found some apartments and most of the apartments came with phone numbers. And some of the phone numbers were United States phone numbers, which kind of flipped me out. How do people have United States phone numbers and they live in Mexico? But anyway, I started calling people. It ended up that many of these people that were renting apartments were Americans or Canadians and they gave me all kinds of information about how they had these phone numbers, what it was like living in Mexico. I could ask them about high speed Internet, so I really needed high speed Internet to support Go to Meeting and all of my Internet adventures.

So that's what happened. I found an apartment, I made my first month rent and my last month rent all through PayPal, grabbed some clothes, my computer equipment and I moved to Puerto Vallarta, Mexico. Now, I was very lucky in that process, I had no problems. The plane landed, I had my clothes, my computer equipment, the taxi took me right to the address of the apartment. I told the people where I was moving into that I needed high speed Internet the day after I got there. So at 10 o'clock the next day in the morning the Internet people showed up, installed my modem and I was working that day. I got there one day, enjoyed the beach for the evening, the next day I was online working and charged my client the next day via PayPal and the money went into my bank account.

That's how I got to Mexico. So in this book, in

this audio tape, what I'm going to share with you is what I have learned in my 12 years of living here. And to be able to look back, I was very lucky about the apartment I got, where it was located, my internet access. But I want to share with you how to do it even more efficiently, so that you can run your business, not have any problems, make money, live comfortably and not worry about anything and really enjoy your life. Again, this is Bill the Geek, *American Living Large in Mexico, Part Two, Planning the Move*.

Chapter 2 – How Much Spanish?

Chapter two. How much Spanish do you need to know?

Well, this is a very good question. And it's a question that must be in your mind, thinking oh, I'm going to be in an all foreign country, everybody's going to be speaking Spanish, I don't know any Spanish. What am I going to do? Well, the answer to that question is you really don't need to know any Spanish, zilch, zero in Spanish "nada". You can live down here and not know or speak any Spanish at all. So don't worry about it, get it out of your head and let me give you some examples. Now, for me, I've been studying Spanish since I was in 7th grade so I got kind of good at Spanish because that's five years of high school going to classes. Then I studied it in college, then in college I went to Mexico on an exchange program and lived with a family where I was supposed to speak Spanish, which I did. And it really did help my Spanish. But I was 19 then and by the time I got to Mexico, I was like 49 years old, that's like a 30-year gap. I don't know, the math's good on that, but that's a 30-year gap. So I forgot about almost all my Spanish by the time I got here. Spanish is a somewhat complicated language because they have different verbs for the past, the present and the future and the verbs change, I'm going to call it to "freaky" terms, because you may have words, you may have rules that apply to this verb universally, but there are all types of verbs that are unique, so you have to know the past, the present and the future for these particular verbs, that you might use all the time.

But anyway, forget about that. Learning Spanish is a good thing. But when I lived in Puerto Vallarta, I knew a woman, she was 75 years old, she had lived in Vallarta for 40 years, she spoke no Spanish, none. Okay? My second landlord or the third landlord, I had in Puerto Vallarta, he owned a home there, a fabulous home, it was fantastic. He was a gay guy, lived with his married partner and neither one of them spoke any Spanish. It's because there are many Mexicans that speak English and what you do is for your services like at the phone company you can find people that speak English. For people that may perform services for your house you find the ones that speak English. Many Americans hang out together, they all speak English and they share attorneys, doctors, dentists, they'll ask one another "Do you know any dentists that speak English? Do you know any doctors that speak English? Do you know any house cleaners that speak English? Who speaks English?" So they just developed this whole community of English speaking people.

So the fact of the matter is almost all Mexicans speak some level of English. Some of it is very limited English. All Mexicans know what okay means and if you speak very slowly in English, most Mexicans will get the drift of what you mean. Now, I was told that there are more than 360 dialects of Spanish, so even if you know very good Spanish, you will run into people who speak a dialect of Spanish. And even if your Spanish is very good, you'll have no clue what these people are talking about because it's a dialect. And I remember watching television years ago, watching ABC nightly news and they had a sheriff in Kentucky who had made a big drug bust out in the mountains somewhere. And this guy talked, he had a really thick Appalachian accent and it was really... because he was talking like "Well, what happened in the woods...and then we dragged them down", you know, and his English was so different that ABC gave him subtitles. So even in English there are dialects that are hard to understand even if you are a native-born American speaking very good English. The same is true in Mexico.

Now, many Mexicans speak very good English and you may know them for months or even years and they will never speak English to you because you have to develop a trust level. I met, I dated a woman for a year, she never spoke any English. I didn't know she spoke English until after a year. One day she starts speaking fluent English. I say "You speak English?" She says "Yeah." And I said "Well, why didn't you tell me you speak English?" She says "Well, if I spoke to you in English, you wouldn't learn Spanish."

Another incident. I would go to this Taco stand, I was living on the food in this Taco stand for about a year because I didn't know where to shop, where to buy food and this place was cheap, there are Burritos, Quesadilla Asada was magnificent. So I just go there by the food, order the food, take it back to my apartment, eat it there. So after buying food there for like 9 months, all of a sudden the guy behind the counter, who I talk to every day for nine months, starts speaking English. It's like all of a sudden he trusted me or something. And then "Oh, you're an okay guy, I'll speak English with you."

So, you can move here. I know numerous Americans and Canadians live in Mexico, they speak no Spanish at all. And so what you will do is you will find an immigration attorney that speaks fluent English, you'll find doctors that speak fluent English, dentists that speak fluent English and you'll make friends. I've been here 12 years and if you want to learn Spanish, I own Rosetta Stone. Rosetta Stone will really set you up with the basics, terms like "turn left", "turn right", "go straight", "the corner", "where is the corner?", what is the word for the corner, what is the word for bathroom, what is the word for milk, what is the word for eggs, what is the word for a fork, what is the word for a plate, what is the word for a beer, what is the word for "give me the bill." Rosetta Stone will help you learn these 50 words, maybe 20, 20 to 50 words that will help you out. And if you want to go further with the Spanish, then Rosetta Stone would do that also. But if you want to learn Spanish, when you get here, use your Rosetta Stone, but you can hire personal Mexican bilingual Spanish teachers for conversational Spanish. Because you can read Spanish and listen to Rosetta Stone and listen to tapes, but once you get in a group of people and people start talking, Mexicans talk fast and you need to develop your listening conversational skills, so that you can understand the language. Studying the Spanish is one thing, but being able to hear it, when it's spoken quickly, it's another thing. So that's a decision that you'll have to make. So may I say it again? That you can come down here and speak no Spanish at all, but the more Spanish that you learn once you're here, the more Mexicans will open up to you and you will want to make trips away from the office to some of these wonderful little cities and towns where you will want to ask questions and you will want to understand the answers to those questions.

Now, one thing that comes to mind that was very important to me, when I got to Mexico my goal was to make money, build my business, so I didn't have to worry about anything. So as far as studying Spanish over my first 10 years in Mexico, to be very honest I studied no Spanish. My Spanish was...if you're an American and you hear me speak Spanish you would say "oh, you're Spanish." Very good. Ha-ha. But if you're a Mexican and you know Spanish, you'd say "your Spanish is very bad." That's how my Spanish is. And for 10 years my goal was to grow my business because nobody was paying me to learn Spanish, but people were paying me to learn PHP, CSS, HTML, Photoshop, Animation, so I studied that all the time. And I did a lot of marketing and that's how I spent my time. Most of my friends and acquaintances were Americans, so I would hang out with them and just, you know, hang loose.

So I think I've said it three or four times, but don't worry about understanding Spanish to come down here, because you can come down here and not speak any Spanish for the rest of your life down here and be just fine. This is Bill the Geek. Visit my website at billthegeek.com or billthegeek.com/members.

Chapter 3 – Communicating with Mexico from the United States

Well, now it's time to find a place and to get information about telephone company and gas and electric and rent and all of that type of thing. But to do that, you need some form of communication that you can talk to people in Mexico. And this is amazing, this international technology that we have now. I remember when I was 19 living in San Luis Potosi, I had a girlfriend in Columbus, Ohio and for 9 weeks I talked with her briefly on the phone over periods of time "hello, how you doing? da-da-da" and when I left Mexico, the family that I was staying with gave me a phone bill for 600 dollars. That was back in like 1978 around there. But now you can communicate from the United States to Mexico pretty much for free.

So before we go into finding an apartment and getting information and contacting Americans, contacting Canadians that can give you information to help you out, I wanted to come up with some ideas for you on how to communicate with these people for pretty much free and with open access, so that you can call these people whenever you want to, directly with no problems.

Now, when I first called Mexico to find out about apartments and living and all that type of thing, I was fortunate enough to run into an American. He was retired and I called him on an American phone line and I asked him "How is it that you live in Mexico and you have an American phone line?" And he says oh, I have Vonage. Oh, **Vonage** works from the United States to Mexico? He says oh, sure it does. And I used, I paid Vonage 49 dollars a month for probably seven or eight years. And then somebody told me about **MagicJack**.

Well, first of all let's talk about what are the benefits of having an American phone line. Well, as you initiate these contacts, it will be very handy because you can just call their American phone line. But when you get your business going, you want people your clients to have the power to call you and ask you questions from your website, you want people to be able to call you up and say "hey, I'm interested in your business" and they don't know you're in Mexico, they think you're in whatever your area code is that goes with **Vonage**.

So anyway, years later I found out about MagicJack. MagicJack is this little USB port, this is just amazing. MagicJack is a USB port, you stick it into any computer, Mac or PC, you choose what area code that you want. I have a 415 area code. So when prospects go to my website, they look at my phone number, it says 415, well, I'm a geek. So 415 area code for people that could visit my website means that this is like a real geek, because 415 is downtown San Francisco. Okay. So with MagicJack...they sell these things at RadioShack, CVS pharmacy, you buy it. It cost about 49 dollars for the little USB port and may be down to 39 now. And then you pay them 35 dollars a year for the MagicJack service. You can make all the calls you want, you can talk to people for 24 hours a day, for one year, they can be located in Mexico, the United States or Canada and it's going to cost you 35 dollars a year.

The good thing about MagicJack that has changed just within the last two years is now MagicJack supports texting. So people can text you through Magic Jack. MagicJack has a built-in message center, so people can leave you messages on MagicJack. I have MagicJack, I love MagicJack. And many times I'll take trips to these small towns on the beach, I'll be in a fabulous hotel, I have all my computer equipment with me with MagicJack. And the really strange thing about MagicJack is that they have apps for your cell phone, which is another story, Cell phones in Mexico. But I have a Galaxy 7 and my service is through **Telcel**. That is the cell phone company in Mexico, owned by **Carlos Slim**. Carlos Slim is a Harvard graduate, he owns a major stake in New York Times, he owns all of this stuff and he owns most of Mexico. Okay? But anyway, the Telcel is owned by Carlos Slim. But anyway, so I have my Galaxy 7. It's a Mexican phone number, but I have an app with MagicJack, so that when people call my American San Francisco phone number, my Galaxy

7 rings. I don't know how many times I have been in grocery stores or a pharmacy or in the park, my phone rings and it's someone who wants to do classes for my web development. And I can be anywhere and do business and get clients with MagicJack. It's phenomenal. So anyway, if you're really thinking about moving down here, go ahead and sign up for MagicJack and then you can start calling people in Mexico or anywhere in Canada, United States, or Mexico.

Now, my second communication method of great importance is something else and it's called WhatsApp. It's called WhatsApp. It's an app that you put in your cell phone. Almost every Mexican that I know uses WhatsApp. Now, with WhatsApp, it's just a little application you have in the phone and it's great for texting, you can text messages, you can include video clips, you can click the button and it allows you to actually make a phone call, just like a telephone, you hit the button, the other person's phone rings. Next thing you know you're talking to them on the phone. WhatsApp is totally free and I am recording this audio, writing this book and today is July 17th 2017 and as of right now and as like all of the past it's been active, WhatsApp is totally free. You can download it into your Android phone or to an Apple phone device.

So if you don't get MagicJack, just get WhatsApp and then you can call Mexico and it's totally free. And once you get to Mexico, you can communicate with all the people, your doctor, your dentist. My girlfriend, she makes all...she lives...and her family live through WhatsApp. That's how they communicate and it's all free.

Now, the third method of free communication, which is wonderful, but I think it has its limitations, but it's free and that is Skype. Many people have Skype, millions of people have Skype. Skype is a device that you can put into your cell phone, on your laptop or your desktop and you can call people, they can see you, you can see them, you have audio. You have to download the application, it's free, it's somewhat easy to use.

So there are three ways for you to

communicate with Mexico, three ways. Skype is totally free, WhatsApp is totally free. MagicJack is going to cost you initially for the USB application, but after that it's 35 dollars a month. Now, if you are serious and moving down here, you want to buy MagicJack in the United States before you come down here. Because you can't buy MagicJack in Mexico because Telcel and Telmex, the major telephone companies owned by Carlos Slim, will not allow that type of competition to enter Mexico. So even if you don't buy a MagicJack right now, before you cross the border, go to a CVS, the pharmacy, and buy a MagicJack and bring it here with you and it will be up and ready and you'll be ready to communicate with your clients in the United States. And let me say this about MagicJack. With MagicJack you choose your area code. The first time you log in to MagicJack, you're going to stick MagicJack into your computer and it's going to ask you to register, get your credit card number and it's going to ask you what area code do you want. And then you can choose any 212...I have an attorney, I have a Mexican attorney down here, a real estate attorney and she has a 212 area code. How smart is that? That's Manhattan. That's brilliant, okay? But anyway before we start doing our research and searching for apartments and that type of thing, now you have your devices, so that you can initiate your communications.

Chapter 4 – Finding a Place to Stay in Mexico

Well, okay, I see it as two ways to find a place to stay in Mexico. And of course, I may be limiting myself. Way number three is you already know somebody down there, like your grandmother, your cousin and they have a place where you can stay. But perhaps you don't know anybody down there and so I can think of two ways to make this happen.

Way number one is you're just doing searches on the Internet in places for apartments. Way number two is finding ex-pats or Americans or Canadians in Mexico, talking to these people quite frequently, talking to friends of theirs and finding a place, creating kind of a network, before you go down there, of people that you can trust so you can assuredly find a great place to stay.

So let's go through the, I'm going to call it the sterile method of Internet searches and the use of Craigslist. Now, Craigslist is international and you can find Craigslist by going to craigslist.org. And if you're on their web page on a laptop or a desktop, I don't know how this looks on a cell phone, but on a desktop or a laptop in the upper right hand corner there's a little button for International. And you click that, expand it, you'll see Mexico, you click that and expand that and it has the major cities in Mexico. They list about 13 cities. Two or three that I can remember that they list is **Guadalajara, Puerto Vallarta, Veracruz, Monterrey**. And they have more now. So what you want to do is just go there. I loved Puerto Vallarta, it's by the ocean, it's kind of like a Disneyland town, but I loved the heck out of Guadalajara, a lot better. Some people, there's a place near Guadalajara, it's about 40 minutes away, it's called Lake Chapala, there is a large population of Canadians and Americans that live there, but anyway.

So you just want to go to Craigslist, do the click and then once you do the click, look around for pricing. You want to look at pricing, how much are you going to have to pay for an apartment. I had a great apartment in Puerto Vallarta, this was the most I paid in ten years in Vallarta. I was paying 8000 pesos a month, that's about in this day, that's about 470 dollars a month. Now, as you start looking at these prices, some of the prices will be in pesos and you want to check that out when you're looking at the listing because you might see 8000 and say "I'm not paying 8000 dollars a month for rent", but it's pesos. So you want to go to Google and do a search for money converter and there you can type in pesos and it will convert the pesos to dollars and you can see actually what you're going to be spending. Okay. So now apart from Craigslist, you can click on a city, find apartments in that city.

Now apart from that, what you can do is you can go to Google and type in apartments for rent Puerto Vallarta, Mexico. Apartments for rent, Guadalajara Mexico. And there you'll find an assortment of websites in Spanish and English and all of these sites like Craigslist will have pictures of the apartment of the inside, the outside and give you an idea of what's going on.

Now let's talk about the difference between furnished apartments in the United States and furnished apartments in Mexico. In the United States if you get a furnished apartment, it's going to have a couch, it's going to have a table and chairs in the kitchen maybe, it's going to have a refrigerator and a stove and a bed. Okay? That's what it's going to have. Mexico is totally different. In Mexico when they say furnished, they mean that you can walk into this place with a suitcase and of course your laptop and a computer and you don't need anything. And by not needing anything what I mean is furnished in Mexico means you're going to have knives, forks, plates, bowls, coffee cups, glasses, sheets, towels, toaster, microwave. I mean that's the basics of what you're going to have. You're going to have all the stuff except for a toothbrush that you need, so you can just walk in and start cooking stuff that day: pots, pans, spatula. It's going to have all of that stuff. Many places in

Mexico will have internet and cable included. And most of these things will be listed on the website. What does this include? You're going to pay like 5000 pesos a month. What's that going to cover? I know a guy in Puerto Vallarta, he has a two-storey, three-bedroom, a wonderful great location apartment. He's paying 3500 pesos a month which is the equivalent of about 200 dollars a month. It's a great place. So you can get a fantastic place in Mexico for 3500 pesos a month. That's good money in Mexico for Mexicans.

Okay. Now let me go real quick into modems and internet service. You want to have the modem in your apartment. This is very important. You may run into situations where the landlord has a modem in one room and maybe three apartments have access to this modem or perhaps the landlord lives upstairs from you and the modem is in the landlord's apartment and you just kind of get the internet from that apartment. It's going to run good. But what happens in that situation, for you geeks out there, you understand that there are many times when you need to reset the modem. And these many times may only happen once a month, once every two weeks, once every two months, but when it happens unless you can reset the modem if you're working online, you're screwed if you can't reset the modem and if the person where the modem is they're at work, they went on vacation, God forbid, and they won't be back for two weeks. This has happened to me. So you want to make damn sure that whatever agreement you have with the person where you're going to rent, that you have access to the modem and if...whatever...You want a modem in your apartment that you can see and turn on, turn off and reset.

Okay. Now let's go to option number two. Option number two is doing a search on Google for finding Canadians and Americans that live in the cities that you want to live in. So in that case, what you want to do is get on Google and do a search for Americans living in Puerto Vallarta, Canadians living in Puerto Vallarta. Another term for that is ex-pats, expatriates. Ex-pats is a very common term in Mexico. So if you go to Google and type in ex-pats living in Puerto Vallarta, you're going to find several websites, different websites that are newsletters just for Canadians and Americans living in Puerto Vallarta. And it will list different organizations or restaurants owned by ex-pats living in Puerto Vallarta. And some of these places will be bars or restaurants. This is Jimmy's bar or Susie's café. So what you want to do and there'll be a link there, you can go to Susie's café's website…what you want to do is get on the phone and call Susie or call Freddie at Freddie's bar. Now, you may think that these people are total strangers, but the fact of the matter is that whenever you call an English speaking person in these cities that you're calling, many times they will be so happy to speak to you, just because you speak English and they're just so happy to talk to somebody speaking English, that it's actually located in the United States or Canada. And they will spill the beans for you. And if they don't have a lot of time to talk to you, tell them you're looking for an apartment, you're looking to find out more information about the city, do they have time to talk to you or do they know of someone that knows of an apartment, that is renting an apartment, an American or a Canadian that is staying in a place that knows of apartments, of reliable landlords, good places, nice clean places, and these people will talk your ears off. Now, that's way number two. You can go the sterile way in searching websites, run for rental properties or you can do the search and actually find people, make these people your friends over time, they will spill the beans and give you lots and lots of information. And I would suggest, when you get these people on the phone in either methodology, ask them a bunch of questions, ask them what does the apartment have. Another important question is what type of Internet are you going to have. I've mentioned Telmex before. There's Telmex and Telcel. Telcel is for cell phones, Telmex is national Mexico service for landlines and Internet. So when you get Telmex Internet you're going to get a phone, too. You may not use it, but you'll use the Internet. Telmex is the most reliable Internet source. I've never had a problem with Telmex. I used to pay them a 1000 a month. You do the math, it's like 55 dollars a month. Now I have a service in Guadalajara called Izzi, I-Z-Z-I. And it's actually a cable television service, but I pay them 500 pesos a month, so that's like 28 dollars a month for Internet, very reliable, high speed. And not all cities have Izzi. In Puerto Vallarta I had Telecable. Telecable is throughout Mexico. I had a terrible experience with Telecable. I had them for a month, they'd be up a day, down two days, up a day, down two days.

Now, all of these services Telmex, Izzi, Telecable have a different service, depending on where you're living. Other people that I knew in Puerto Vallarta had problems with Telmex because they lived further away from the tower than I did. They lived in great parts of town, but the tower was further away, the signal was set bad and sometimes the signal would turn on and off, thus they would not have internet. You'll have to ask your apartment people how is the internet. This is a very important question. Other things you want to ask the people that you're thinking about moving into for an apartment, you want to ask them are there markets nearby, and when I say markets I'm not talking about supermarkets, but Mexican shop and outdoor markets where you have fresh fruit, fresh vegetables, fresh fish that was caught that day in the sea, fresh pork, fresh beef and the prices are unbelievable. You can go in there and you shop, walk out there with three bags of fish and beef and vegetables and you'll spend like 20 dollars and you'll laugh. When you're leaving, you'll laugh. It is just unbelievable. But you want to ask them about noise also. I know Americans that rented wonderful apartments in downtown Puerto Vallarta and they visited the apartment in the day time. They didn't realize that there was a bar across the street and the bars in Mexico stay open, playing very loud music till 6 o'clock in the morning. You don't want to have that because the music is very loud and you won't be able to sleep. Or you want to ask the people what is the sound situation of the apartment, is there noise or is there no noise. What does the rent include? Does it include water, gas, electricity? Watch out for air conditioning. If it has an air conditioner...air conditioning is one of the most expensive things in Mexico. Everything is cheap in Mexico except for air conditioning. So if you're going to move to Puerto Vallarta, you will need air conditioning, but expect to pay about 400 dollars a month on air conditioning. That's a hell of a lot of money in Mexico. What about cable television? If you're a TV watcher, okay, you get cable TV. Cable TV down here is going to come with like 72 channels, about 40 of those channels are going to be in English: ESPN, CNN, ABC, NBC, CBS, a couple of movie channels and lots of free movie channels. What does it include? Also you're going to want to ask them is there a bank with an ATM within walking distance, is the place new, is it clean, what appliances do you have. I have always in my 12 years in Mexico have had access to a washer and dryer. I don't know if I'm lucky, but it all always worked. But ask them about that. Also ask them where is the closest Oxxo, O-X-X-O. There are 15,000 Oxxo's, they are like 7-Eleven. And in fact, Carlos Slim, I've talked about him before, he owns all the Oxxo's in Mexico. He also owns all the 7-Eleven's and Oxxo's. And then there's this other place called kiosk. They all do the same thing. They're all like 7-Eleven, but he owns all of those, too. But Oxxo is very handy because at Oxxo you can buy all your milk and beer and, you know, dog food, but also you can pay your electric bill, you can pay your gas bill there, you can pay your telephone bill at Oxxo, you can pay for about anything at Oxxo. It's money.

Okay. Now another consideration looking back on things is how long do you want to rent your initial place of stay. I rented my first place for one year. I paid first month rent, last month rent deposit for one year. If I had to do it again, I would have just found a place for two months, I would say okay, I just want to stay there for two months because in two months you can get to know people, walk around town and find out where in town you really want to live. And it will give you time to find a better apartment for a better price. I would think that the goal for your first apartment is just to be comfortable. If you can get lucky and get real comfortable your first time, okay, fine, but I would settle for a clean and appliances and Internet where you can work and be happy, but realize that if in two months you can actually be there and talk to people and see other apartments on the ground, then you can upscale in two months and be much more happy. Now if you're a real freaky deak person, I know a guy who's a retired merchant marine and he comes to Puerto Vallarta for six months every year during the winter when it's the nice weather, meaning that it's 72 degrees every day and blue sky every day with no rain. But he travels the world, all he has is a suitcase. I know the guy makes like 60,000 a year in retirement, but he looks like a bum and he just comes to Vallarta, he doesn't do anything upfront. He just shows up, goes to some hotel or something, checks in and he just stays there six months and it's really inexpensive. Some hotels have monthly rates that are very inexpensive and he just drinks beer all day and sits on the beach. That's what he does. So that's another option.

Now something else to consider is how are you going to pay your rent. Are you going to pay in dollars or are you going to pay in pesos? This is something that should be asked and considered by you upfront. If you're going to pay in dollars, the dollar is fairly steady in value over time. When I first moved to Mexico ten years ago, 10 pesos were worth 1 dollar. Okay, fine. So that means pretty much that 500 dollars is 5000 pesos. Okay. But the

Mexican peso took a hit about three years ago and now 20 pesos equals 1 dollar. So what that means is as an American, I make American dollars, I don't earn any pesos, so everything is half price, everything's been half price down here for me for like 3 years. In other words, if you were renting a place for 5000 pesos three years ago, that would be 500 dollars. But now 5000 pesos is worth 250 dollars. So now you're paying half price on your rent. Now on the bad side of bad, if you come down here and you start paying 8000 pesos, which is about 450 dollars, but then the value of the peso goes up back where it was ten years ago, well that 450 dollars turns into 900 dollars a month. So if you were paying dollars for rent, you wouldn't have a problem. But if you pay in pesos for rent, you have to watch what the currency is doing at the time.

Okay. So now another consideration is for when you're moving into the apartment, how is that payment situation go down. It's pretty customary, it's very customary to pay first month rent, last month rent. Some people ask for first month rent, last month rent and a deposit also. And the deposit is generally the value of one month's rent. Some people will just ask you for one month's rent.

Pretty much those are the options and those are the issues I see with finding your first apartment in Mexico. So that's it for finding your first apartment in Mexico. I hope you're picking up some information and I'll see you in Chapter 5.

Chapter 5 – Learning About Your City or Town

Well I guess when I showed up in Mexico, I guess I was kind of an ugly American because I didn't do hardly any study. I put everything into my work. I tried to ignore Puerto Vallarta. When I first moved to Mexico, gosh, I was living two blocks from the beach downtown Puerto Vallarta which is just like a little blip, a little place called Old Town with a bunch of bars. And the bars were right on the beach, it was so beautiful, it was so wonderful and beautiful that I just had to stay away from it because that would only be trouble. So I just stayed in my apartment and worked a lot but one thing I would do every morning is get up early in the morning, walk down to the beach to a place called **Dee's Café**. And Dee is a Canadian, she makes all of her pastries from scratch every morning at 6.30 and her coffee was so wonderful. She's still there. If you go to Puerto Vallarta, go to Dee's Café and tell her that Silly Billy sent you. Silly Billy is my pen name for when I used to write children's books. But anyway, I really enjoyed that, buy two cups of coffee at Dee's Café and sit on the beach and watch the ocean, a beautiful experience every day one of the benefits of living in Puerto Vallarta, living in Mexico.

But talking about learn about your city or town, what I should've done is learn about the city and the town. And things that come to mind are when are the holidays. Mexico has many holidays. And I mean, they have a lot of holidays, they have three different Independence days, then they have all, but then they have like around Easter everybody's off. Holidays can change your life experience, if you don't know when they are. Because all the banks close, certain services close and air traffic situations change. And your neighbors are all excited because it's a holiday, but you don't know what it is. So find out! And you can just get on the Internet, go to Google and type in Mexican holidays. They'll list them all there. And also when are the festivals. Mexicans have wonderful festivals where farmers come into the city, where you are with their horses and their families and they have these wonderful parades with the horses dancing to music and so and it's beautiful to be a part of the festivals. Also you might want to look up, do a Google search on the history of the city or the town where you are. Do a Google search on museums and places to go in the town where you are. And look at the map! Look at the map and see what small towns are around the city where you're going to go.

Bus services are wonderful in Mexico. To go from Puerto Vallarta to Guadalajara, which is a five-hour drive, it takes five hours to get there in the bus, it only cost about $28 and the buses are fabulous. The buses have cable television, so you can watch an assortment. You can choose from like eight to ten movies to watch on the trip. The buses have Wi-Fi so you can be on your computer working and they're luxurious and clean with the cleanest bathrooms I've ever experienced in my life on a bus. So find out where the towns are, what they have to offer. If you don't have a car, you can take a wonderful bus ride down there, maybe stay in a hotel overnight, take the bus ride back. And in your town find out the major streets. Get on Google! Google is so good about maps internationally, because you'll want to know how to get around and you'll need, like where's the bank, what's on this street, where is this, where is that. Find out from your apartment where is the nearest hospital. These are things and what you want to do is know and you want to visit the hospital and see the hospital, so you know where the hospital is and take down the main phone number of the hospital. Most of the hospitals in Mexico have nurses or coordinators that speak English. Find out who this person is because emergencies are emergencies and that's something that you want to know. Where is the dentist, where is the doctor? I've been very fortunate in all of my locations. Currently my dentist is two blocks away and he speaks fluent English and unfortunately I've had to see him about eight times in the last month, for good things, you know, repair this, repair that. Dentists are like really cheap down here. I mean you can get your teeth cleaned for like $28 and crowns and all that stuff is really cheap. But where's the dentist? What is your dentist's phone number? What is his WhatsApp connection phone number?

Where is the pharmacy? Pharmacies are great down here. Many pharmacies have doctors. If you get a cold or this or that, you go visit the doctor at the pharmacy, he checks you out, says this or that and that's only going to cost you like $5 to talk to the doctor. He gets the stethoscope, puts a thermometer in your mouth, ta-ta-ta. Okay. And then, you're at the pharmacy, so you go buy some pharmacy drugs that are really cheap also. You know, where is the nearest doctor?

What is the police phone number? What is the ambulance phone number? You may live in a place that is a little bit the same, maybe it's 15 blocks away from the big grocery store. In a big grocery store, they have a place called **Soriana or Mega** or in Puerto Vallarta and Guadalajara they have **Costco**. I have a car, so I can drive to Costco in like four minutes. But if I didn't have a car and I'd buy a lot of stuff at Costco, I'd need a taxi. Taxis are really cheap, really really cheap. But it's nice if you have their phone number. In Guadalajara they have Uber, which is cheaper than the taxi and the cars are a lot nicer and it's really nice to order the Uber to come visit you on your cell phone because you can see when they're going to get there. You can actually see their car in Uber in your cell phone. Very reliable. Old towns do not have Uber in Mexico. But having the phone number of the taxi is very handy if you need to go for a distance more than eight blocks and you don't feel like walking.

Another thing strongly that I suggest is where is the closest United States Embassy. If you're Canadian, where is the closest Canadian embassy. You never know when your passport needs renewal, you have to go to the embassy. So I would actually go and visit the embassy, get all of the embassy's information. If you can, set an appointment to meet with the director of the embassy. Now it sounds like a very official position, but the embassy in Puerto Vallarta, they probably have like eight people that work there. It's not like a big group of people and they're just normal people. And the director of the embassy in Puerto Vallarta is just this real laid back lady, that's just happy to be living in Puerto Vallarta, doing what she's doing. If you have a legal problem or, God forbid, end up in jail, because you're an asshole in a bar or something, you're going to need to talk to the embassy. I've never had that problem. But go visit the embassy, ask for an appointment with the director just to say "hello, I'm here, I plan on being here in a while", make a good impression on the director. You never know what might happen in a foreign country and when you may need the embassy's help. And lastly what is the embassy's phone number, and when you're talking to the director of the embassy or perhaps you end up just talking to a staff member at the embassy, what numbers do you call after hours should the embassy be closed. But be a good American, do your research, what are the holidays, what are the street names, where's the hospital, where's the local dentist, where's the closest doctor, get to know the community and you won't run into problems down the road.

Chapter 6 – You Are All Moved in. Leave the Apartment.

Okay. So you've rented a place, you've traveled a ton, you've moved your stuff in, hopefully you don't have too much. Your apartment is okay, at least for a couple of months or maybe for a year. Now it's time to see what your neighborhood has to offer. Mexico is a very strange place and one thing I love about Mexico is the way of life down here is so different, that from one day to another you're going to see things that you just won't believe, things that would be illegal in the United States. Just wait and see. And illegal in a nice way. Go out and walk this way down your street for like five blocks, go that way down your street, five blocks, go to the corner, turn left and go five blocks, go to the corner and turn right and go five blocks. Do the same thing for the corner on the reverse sides and do that frequently until you expand your knowledge of the neighborhood. The little shops in Mexico are very specific. I remember one shop in Puerto Vallarta, they only sold trash bags and they sold trash bags by the leader. A block away from here there's a place, it's a **Cremeria**. In English that would be a cream shop, but what it means in Mexico is cheeses. They have all kinds of cheeses and it's a little small place, about half the size of a bedroom, but they have all kinds of cheeses, bacon... This lady sells fresh eggs from farms, not like Oxxo or the grocery store, but she has farmers from the country bringing the eggs and she sells eggs by the kilo. So when I go there and I buy eggs, I say I want one kilo of eggs. One kilo of eggs is about fourteen eggs. That's the Cremeria. But the only way you're going to find these places is by getting out of the apartment and just walking around. They have a place that only do copies of things, on the computer.

Also the little places to eat. The little places to eat will be very surprising for you because most of them won't look very fancy and you'll see many cart vendors. Some carts are there all of the time. These little white places with a place to cook and then they'll have these plastic chairs around them, most of them say Corona on the back and then they'll have little tables with a little red tablecloth on them. And Americans are very snobbish because they're so used to going into McDonald's or Burger King, even though you can go down here also, but these places look very different. And I've eaten at many of these places and I've never gotten sick. Many of these little outdoor...they're very strange looking, but they have excellent food and many of them have been there for like 30-40 years in their family places and they cook family traditional Mexican food with fresh tortillas. Fresh tortillas to make tacos, quesadillas. They're cooking things with onion and hot peppers and special sauces, they all have fresh guacamole and tomatoes and other things. So look around and see it...because when you're hungry in the middle of the night or late in the early evening, perhaps you just want to go get something and the prices are unbelievably reasonable. You can go spend $3 at one of these places and get so much food that you won't be able to eat it all. It's phenomenal. But get to know your neighborhood and as you walk around from block to block to block, make a notation "Oh, this place sells this, this place sells that, this little place sells this and this and this." It's so different. It's a **Wal-Mart** within where I live in Guadalajara in ten minutes I can get to like four or five different Wal-Marts. They have two Wal-Marts that I know of in Puerto Vallarta. And Wal-Mart is such a business crusher, that's what Wal-Mart does. Wal-Mart goes into a place, opens up, they sell everything very somewhat inexpensive and they put tons of small businesses out of business. That hasn't taken its full effect in Mexico as yet. So Mexico, prior to Wal-Mart, was just a bunch of little shops supplying neighborhoods. And in all of these little teeny-tiny restaurants that are on the street on the corner you're going to find Juiceria, places that will juice things up for you: watermelon, cantaloupe. It's traditional to put hot sauce in your watermelon juice or your cantaloupe juice. This will be on the corner.

I buy **tamales** regularly from this guy. His wife makes the tamales and he stands in front of Oxxo. This place is like nine blocks away, he's there most days, he doesn't sell them on Mondays, but they're excellent. Tamales, it's really weird. He has like a little cooler and he's got his tamales, he has different flavors of tamales: tamales with chicken, tamales with pork, tamales for vegetarians, tamales with cheese, without cheese, spicy tamales, mild tamales and they're excellent. Tamales are cooked in this special leaf. You put this special, some kind of tree leave, I don't even know what kind of tree… my girlfriend knows what it is. And that adds flavors to the tamales, but it's special.

There's a guy that comes regularly to the corner, half a block away in front of this Oxxo. Now, that Oxxo, I can walk to like five Oxxo's in five minutes. The closest one is like a half a block away. I can walk there in like two minutes. Oxxo's are everywhere. You might see two Oxxo's and one block. They're kind of like Starbucks in the United States. But anyway, this guy shows up at 8.30 on the corner every night. He has tamales. Sometimes he'll have corn. Corn in a plastic cup. You'll find that a lot down here. You want some corn in a plastic cup and they have a special sauce, they put on it, sell it to you for like, you know, veinte pesos, 20 pesos, that's like 90 cents. Okay.

But as you walk around, you know, you've moved into your apartment, get out! Be comfortable! Find out what your neighborhood has to offer that will enhance your life. Being an American, if you're coming to Mexico for the first time, it's a show every day because you're going to see a new way of life every day and around every corner there's going to be something that's going to freak you out and you're going to say "What? What?" And it's a wonderful thing. It will add new spices to your life.

Chapter 7 – Your Bank

Money is going to be your lifeline to survival down here. Everything can go well, good and fine but if your money is funny, then life can be quite challenging, scary and miserable and that is far away from happy. So my lifeline to my money is my bank account and the people who handle my money, so I can get my money when I want my money. This is very important. And I rely heavily on my ATM card. I guess I spend a lot of money on business expenses, usually that is through PayPal, sometimes through my United States bank account, but generally to get food and just to buy some gasoline down here, I need cash. Okay? So I always have about 10,000 pesos. I always have about 10,000 pesos access to that. I should make that about...I should up that. I should up it so that I always have access to about 30,000 pesos and I have that in the house so that if there is an emergency and I need to get the heck out of Mexico, then I can go to the airport and get a ticket, a plane ticket out of here and not have to worry about that.

And I hadn't planned on writing or talking about that, but that is something very important. Come down here, buy a safe. Buy a safe that's heavy and there are a lot of safe shops down here. Buy a safe and keep 30,000 pesos in there so that if the ship goes down and you have to get out of town, you can just go to the airport and get the hell out of here. Okay?

But let's talk about money. I would think before you come down here...the shop banks in the United States. Get on the Internet and shop what is a good bank to have, if you're an American living in Mexico. For like nine years I used US Bank and I used them before I moved to Mexico. In fact, I started using them in the year 2000 when I lived in San Francisco, that's where I opened the account, in San Francisco. So I had been with them pretty much for 16 years. The downside of US Bank was they charged me every month, they would charge me $6 for a maintenance fee. I don't know what that was for and then every time I went to the ATM, they charged me $15 for an international withdrawal fee and then I had to pay...I'm paying US Bank $15 to take my money out, then I'm getting charged $2.5 by the ATM for the Mexican bank. So that's like $17.5, I'm only allowed to take out 6,000 pesos at a time, that's only like $300. So, you know, I'm paying

$17 to take out $300. You do that a couple of times a month, three times a month, that's like $45 just in banking fees. And then what happened was I'm sitting down here minding my own business after sixteen years with the US Bank, they send me a letter and they tell me that they don't want my money anymore because I live in Mexico. Well, okay, what the heck is that? That freaked me out. I'm in Mexico, I have to find a new American bank, which like just freaked me out. Okay? And I had a substantial amount of money in the bank. Okay.

You don't want me and I have money? Okay? So what I did was I opened an account with **Charles Schwab.** Now, Charles Schwab has an international account that you can open, with no ATM fees, which is pro-great, okay? No ATM fees. So now the catch is to open that account you need $25,000 dollars in the bank. But I would think...so you need to open it with 25,000 and then if the amount goes down, you're okay. You open it with 25,000 and then if it ends up going down to 2,000, they don't care, but you have to have 25,000 to get in there. So if you don't have 25,000, but your mom, your dad does or your cousin does and you just want to open the account with 25 grand, then kick back your cousin like 20 grand, you've got 5 grand in the bank then that will cut out your ATM fees.

Charles Schwab is wonderful, their customer service is wonderful, you can call them on the phone, take care of anything. But that is a consideration finding a reliable bank that is not going to charge you money out the ass every time you go to the ATM machine and then monthly services for maintenance fees. Now when you get here and you're going to use your ATM card, I only go to one bank and that bank is about a half a mile away from here. I have to drive there, but I like this bank because you stick the card in, but the card doesn't go all the way in it. There's a little click and you can see the card, you get your money out and then there's a click and the little machine says "take your card" and then you take your card and then it gives you your money. Okay. What I like about that is many machines down here, you put your card in, the card goes into the machine and a couple of times when I used that methodology, the machine took my card which is a pain in the butt because not all Mexican banks will give you your card back, depending upon the location of the bank. It may be a central system where they have to call special people down and you have to visit the bank like five times to get your card back and you're trying to negotiate this in Spanish because not all people in the bank and not all banks have people that speak English in the banks and it can be a very pain in the butt situation. So in Puerto Vallarta there was a bank, I only went to one bank for my money in this situation you stick the card in and the card goes into the machine, but the way that the money machine was set up it's in the door of the bank. And if it took my card then I could go into the bank, they had a lady that was a manager that spoke English and I could say "the machine took my card" and she walks into the machine, she walks into the room where the back of the machines are and she can grab my card and give it back to me. Okay. You may think that I'm obsessing about this, but something happens to your ATM card and that is your money. That's where you get your money to buy your groceries, to take care of emergencies, to go to the doctor, just to get some milk. That thing disappears, then you have to rely upon your bank in the United States to get you a new card, which in a good situation you're going to have a new card from your bank, they'll Federal Express it, DHS it down here and you can have it in three days, four days a week if your bank is a good bank. Okay? If your bank is not a good bank, it may take a month. I was in that situation with the US Bank and it took me a month to get a new card. So the ATM machine situation is very important.

Also there are people in Mexico, you go to an ATM machine, you put your card in and then the person behind you is a thief. They have these special little devices that they follow you after you put your card in, they put in a special card which records your transaction along with all of the information from your ATM card, so by following you inserting this device in, taking your information all of a sudden they have your...in essence, they have your ATM information. And I know many Americans and Canadians this has happened to and all of a sudden they're getting notices from their bank that their card has been used in like, you know, literally seven to thirteen places within an hour of that happening, with charges up to like $3,000.

So now all Oxxo's and many places have ATM machines, so you have to find if you're going to live down here, live in a neighborhood, you need to find a secure ATM machine. In Puerto Vallarta, the ATM machine that I was talking about, it was at a bank, it was in the door of the bank. The bank had a security guard in front of the ATM all of the time. The bank that I go to now has a security guard in front of the ATM all the time. I would never use an ATM in Oxxo or 7-Eleven. I don't even use the ATM in Costco. Okay? So I think that is a very important consideration.

Another important consideration in banking, I would definitely shop for banks that can provide... US banks or United States banks that can provide you with good service when you're in Mexico. I would suggest, before you leave, if you're going to stick with your existing bank, go down to your bank and talk to the branch manager and say "Hey, I'm moving to Mexico and I want to know who you are, I want to know your name", because should something happen to your card, should the bank send you a letter with some alarming information about your account, you're going to have to call special people at your bank. And many times it comes down to you're going to need to talk to the branch manager. And if you don't know who that is, then you have to find that person on the fly and the person doesn't know who you are. So you want to make a relationship with the branch manager of your bank, if it's nothing but you going to the bank where you opened your account. That's very important also. Many times it comes down to where did you open your account. And you want to talk to the branch manager there and let that person know who you are, so that you can call them if your card ends up stolen, God forbid, or sucked up in some machine and you need a new one, so that this person remembers you. And if you tell the branch manager that you're moving to Mexico, that is something that they will remember because not a lot of people do that. And you want to kind of stay in touch with this person so that if they are promoted or fired or moved to a new location, then you need to find out who is replacing them and you need to make a relationship with them.

Now, as far as Mexican banks go, Mexican banks are strange. Mexican banks are not customer friendly. I'm going to say it kind of seems like Mexican banks are a sham. I would never put my money in a Mexican bank, I'm sorry. They charge you. If you deposit more than a certain amount, then they want a percentage of the amount that you deposited. Also, I think it's on a yearly basis, they want to charge you a fee for the money that you keep in your bank account and the government wants to tax you money on the money that you have in the Mexican bank account. So personally, I had a Mexican bank account with maybe $100 and thought it would be convenient. I don't use that. I don't have any money in Mexican banks, I don't do any electronic Mexican business. All of my money is in the United States or PayPal. So I think that is all of the considerations that I have for banking. But make a relationship with your bank before you move down here and then once you get down here, be very careful with the use of your ATM card.

Chapter 8 – Mail Service

This isn't going to be a lengthy chapter. I don't have much to say, but in Mexico mail service is very strange. It is nothing at all like the United States. Another thing, one thing that I didn't say is when you move into your apartment places to look for like the doctor, the hospital, that type of thing you also want to find out where is the Postal Service. The postal services here are nothing like the United States. The locations...so much of Mexico is so modern. You can go in the hospitals, restaurants, places of business and it looks more sophisticated than the United States: banks, Burger King, okay. But you go into any post office in Mexico, it's like you're stepping back in time about 100 years and you don't get mail every day. You never know when your mail is going to show up, you don't have a postman who walks door to door every day, your mail shows up, some guy will usually come on a motor scooter and, you know, usually it's for bills. He's giving people electric bills, this, that. If somebody sends you mail from the United States, you may never get it. If you do get it, it's going to show up at like a month to six weeks from the time that they sent it. I had a cousin that was getting married like on last year on July 15th, the family sent me that invitation in April and I didn't get the invitation until August, which was two weeks after the wedding. It took that particular letter way longer than it needed to. Okay? You do the math!

So I never send anything through the mail here because if you send something it may never show up. If somebody sends you something, you may never get it. And in Chapter 7 I was talking about my banking situation with the US Bank and they didn't have a service, they wanted to send me a card and put it in the mail and I was telling...they wanted to send me an ATM card and put it in the mail. I said "You don't want to send me an ATM card to Mexico because I don't know when I ever get it. Can you send it to Federal Express?" Well, they said "Well, no, we can't do that. We don't have a service that offers that." That's another banking consideration in an emergency situation. Can they send you a card through an overnight service that services Mexico? But anyway...

So when I need to send something important to the United States I use DHL. DHL is like the balm down here. They also have Federal Express here. Federal Express, DHL, they have all of the major overnight services. So I follow my taxes every year and for tax situations I go down to DHL, I have to pay them about $45 to send in my tax information. But with that comes the tracking information. I can track it day by day to make sure that the IRS received it and that they signed off on it. Occasionally, I've had deaths in the family where I had to sign documents electronically and then send them overnight. DHL is the way to go. So I never use the mail service unless it's something very important and in those cases it's always overnight services, DHL, UPS works, all of those are down here. But when you come down here, you may as well forget about regular mail. If you send anything through the Mexican mail system, it's almost like just throw it right in the garbage, you don't know if they're going to get it, you don't know when they're going to get it. That's...I mean, of all the fabulous things in Mexico, I mean, as modern and wonderful as it is, I don't know what's up with the postal service. So you can forget about that! Forget about mail, okay? Just forget about it!

Chapter 9 – Eating Out. What to Expect.

Mexico has many fine restaurants that you can go to or many times you will end up eating on the street at these little restaurants that are in the street or these little places that really don't look like restaurants, but it just has an open front area and there are tables inside and they're cooking in the back. You'll see when you get here, okay? But they all have a few things in common. And what I find interesting is the billing situation.

When they bring you the cheque and how and when you order food? Now at many of the taco stands you may go to it's totally different than the United States. It's like you might want this kind of taco, then you want a different kind of taco, then maybe you want something else, then maybe you want a beverage and maybe you want a this and that. So they don't visibly keep track of what you're doing, apparently they are. And they all operate the same way. This can be a very fancy restaurant or this can be a-hole-in-the-wall place or it can be a street vendor place. And they're very friendly about you taking your time, enjoying the food and never rushing the money experience. So you know, it's kind of sit there and it's totally different than McDonald's. You go to McDonald's and you order this and that and that, they want the money right now, then you can eat the food.

In the Mexican restaurant situation you just kind of sit there and "I'll have one of these tacos or I want one of those tacos, give me one of those fruit drinks." Oh, okay, da-da-da…and you just sit there and in twelve years I can't remember ever ever ever them ever asking me "Do you want the cheque now?" Never. I always have to ask for the cheque, which for some reason that annoys me a little bit. It's like "Okay, I'm done. Can I have the cheque? Please bring me the cheque." You always have to wave them down. Please let me pay you now, because I'm done. Okay? But in a way that's very hospitable, no rush. Okay. Eat what you want, when you want, to take your time and when you're ready to pay, let us know and we'll bring you the cheque. And that's the way it is. That's a little weird for me. Maybe with you, you'll just drop right in with the program.

Now for you drinkers out there, for you people that drink beer or mixed drinks, something that really annoys me down here, if you go into a restaurant and you order a beer, you're going to get your beer at an excellent price. You're going to get a really nice beer for like 90 cents, $1.25. It's almost standard. And beers on tap down here, where they go to the tap, put your beer in a glass, that's very rare. Almost all the time you're going to get your beer in a bottle, they're going to have like three to fifteen types of beers that you can order and it's going to be a very standard fair price. When it comes to mixed drinks, like a Tom Collins or Martini, something like that, you're going to get screwed on that. I don't know what the deal is down here, but as soon as you want a mixed drink, a Bacardi and this, Tanqueray and that, they're going to want to charge you like $5 for that. And Tequila! You order some tequila and especially if you're an American or Canadian, because then it seems like this little red light goes off in their heads, like "Oh, you want, oh, you're an American, you want some tequila, okay, this shot of tequila is going to cost you like $7.

I was at a place a month ago in downtown Guadalajara. Guadalajara has some fabulous places to visit. And it's a famous famous restaurant and it's actually about five restaurants around the periphery of this big…Gazebo and Mariachi bands play there all day. And it's a must-see if you visit Guadalajara. All of the furniture…the place is about the size of half of a football field and all of the tables and chairs are all wood, leather antique. The place is beautiful and they have a special tequila drink that they serve in a bowl with ice and fruits. Okay?

So the bowl isn't really that big but, you know, the people that I was with said "Well, you're here and you really have to get this at least once." And so I said "Okay, very good." And that drink was 400 pesos, which is like $22. I didn't know it when I ordered it, but $22 in Mexico and maybe it had a shot of tequila in it with some fruit juice. No!!! Okay?

Or I was in another situation, in a very nice hotel on the beach in Puerto Vallarta in the evening, I mean it's a very exclusive restaurant and the waiter says "Oh, we have a special drink tonight, this, this, that." "Okay, I said, okay fine." But what he didn't tell us was that for this very small, it was almost like a shot glass worth of a drink and that drink was like 300 pesos which is like $16 and me and my girlfriend...so it's like two shots of something...something for like $32.

So when you go into the restaurant, take your time, eat your food, ask for the cheque when you're ready, but be aware of...I never order mixed drinks in a restaurant because the prices, unless you have tons and tons of money you want to give away, but for the money that they're charging for a drink in a restaurant, you could buy two or three fifths of the alcohol and just stay at home. But anyway, that's my humble tip on what to expect in restaurants, the eating experience in Mexico.

Chapter 10 – Jobs You Can Have in Mexico

Well, jobs you can have in Mexico. If you don't have an online business and come down here, your feet are on the ground and you're ready to make money online. If you want to work in a Costco or an Oxxo or get a not so well-paying job and you just want to live on that to pay your rent, I'm going to say upfront, just don't think about it! Because Mexicans don't earn a lot of money. Per capita income down here is $9000 a year, so the person that works eight to ten hours and seven and eleven is earning about 15 to 20 dollars a day. In the United States, you know, they're trying to get to $15 an hour or $9 an hour, or $7 an hour is the minimum wage. That's not going on down here. Policemen only make about $20 a day, they have one uniform, they take it home and clean it every night, they share guns. When you get off of your shift you leave your gun, the next person on the shift takes the gun. If you shoot your gun and you didn't kill anybody, you have to pay for the bullets that you use. If you have a construction job, you may work eight to ten hours in a day for 10 dollars.

Mexicans do not make money. Thus, Mexican businesses do not pay money. School teachers make about $180 week. Most Mexican businesses and people that work for Mexican businesses have six-day work weeks and they're off one day, which is Sunday. And I've met people who have, Mexicans that have security jobs in really fancy resorts and they may work six days a week, eight hours a day and that pays about $180. So if you come down here with no skills, no online businesses, you may be able to get a "okay" job as a bartender. Then you can only work and live on tips or a waitress or perhaps a hostess, but in those situations you will have to speak some Spanish. If you're a hostess or a waitress, you just have to know the words on the menu, but still you need to know some Spanish to do those jobs. Now in Puerto Vallarta I knew many Americans without jobs that needed money, who would sell timeshares. The timeshare business in Puerto Vallarta is huge. Some people sell timeshares and they make very good money and you don't have to know any Spanish because you have Canadians and Americans visiting the timeshare places, and these visitors give them $100 just to go through the timeshare interview system. And I have met and I know some people that make really good money selling timeshares. Now I know a retired attorney, that lived in my neighborhood in Puerto Vallarta, he was a retired attorney, I don't know if he just quit his job or whatever, he was sick of the legal industry in the United States...what he does, he watches cars, he goes around the neighborhood, he has regular clients that every such and such a day he knows to go to this person's house and wash their car. I mean, this guy has a law degree and that's how he makes money. He's very good with it. It's regular, the money's okay, washing a car for like $3.5, get another car, okay.

So if you come down here with no job skills and you can't speak Spanish, you can't even work at 7-Eleven because you have to know the Spanish behind the computers and be able to speak with the customers in Spanish. I mean you can't even get a low level job if you don't speak fluent Spanish. Now on the other hand, if you hook up...I know Americans that speak no Spanish or limited Spanish that hook up with Canadians or Americans that own hotels or own tourist services or tourist food tours and they market internationally those services, you can hook up with American or Canadian business owners and only speak English and make some money if you can help them market the business and make money like that. But if you're thinking about coming down here and getting a Mexican job, working for a Mexican business... You can come down and do plumbing or electricity, but it pays no money.

Now I have a very very good friend who is a very good auto mechanic from Oregon. And this guy, he's like a genius, on many different aspects of life, he can work on any car, he's very good, he knows computer systems and cars and he lives in Puerto Vallarta, his name is Doug. And this guy... this is a very interesting story. He rents an apartment on the corner, where there's a Mexican auto mechanic shop and it's somewhat an upscale Mexican auto mechanic shop. Doug only services cars for Canadians and Americans in Puerto Vallarta and he charges good money. Now, the thing about a car, when you have a problem with a car and you don't speak Spanish, how are you going to tell the auto mechanic what's wrong with your car and when he does a diagnosis and knows what's wrong, how are you going to know what he's saying when he's telling you what's wrong with your car. The good situation about Doug is he pays the auto mechanic repair shop for him to be able to go there and use their tools, their hydraulic lift and all that kind of stuff and he keeps their place full of Americans and Canadians that need work, because Doug speaks Spanish and English and he's very good. He has a gig going on. If you're an auto mechanic and you can hook up with a place like this, it's very easy to do, you can make a good living working only with Americans and Canadians that need work on their car. That is a very unique situation.

Things that you can do, you can make a business, if you're bilingual, you can make a business of teaching Americans and Canadians Spanish. You don't want to teach Mexicans how to speak English because they don't want to pay you, they want to pay you maybe like a Mexican wage. You might do two hours of classes with a Mexican speaking English, teaching them English, but then they're only going to want to pay you maybe $3 for two hours. On the other hand if you're teaching a Canadian or an American Spanish, you can charge them $20 to $30 an hour. So that's a market also.

I have a friend down here who is a school teacher. If you're bilingual and you are a school teacher, you can teach at school down here but you don't want to teach at a regular Mexican public school. You want to teach in a private school and there are many Mexican private schools down here, but you don't want to teach in one of those regular private schools. You want to teach in an American or an international school. That's where the rich Mexicans send their kids to go to school and you can make a reasonable income working there. It's not going to be like being a teacher in New York City. In New York they pay their teachers like $50,000 to 75,000 a year. It's going to be nowhere near that, but it's going to pay more money than any environment. And if you love teaching, you can do that down here in Mexico. You can get on the Internet, do a search for international schools, they are always looking for Americans and Canadians that are very good at teaching and that are bilingual.

But my suggestion is get your online business together, come down here with your online business, go in and work in your apartment. So the following chapters are going to be mostly about your online business, marketing your online business, what types of online businesses to think about, search engine optimization, creating your website, managing your website, getting customers to call you, getting new clients to find you on the Internet, setting up your Pay Pal account, billing people through your website, so that you're making substantial dollars that Mexicans wouldn't even believe the kind of money that you're making. I charge $45 an hour for my web development, search engine optimization consulting and it was about probably about eight years ago the restaurant owner around the corner asked me "How much money do you make doing this?" And I said "$45 an hour" and he about died, it was a shock for him. Someone making $45 an hour was shocking, he was shocked. Okay? I never ever told anyone how much I make an hour ever again down here. But you can do consulting through the Internet and make $45, at least $25 an hour and up sitting in your apartment. And those are the issues that we will go in into the next chapters.

Chapter 11 – What Online Business Can You Make Happen.

Well, very briefly I'm going to share with you how I make money online and why. Every dime that I've made for the last twelve years has come from online business. People want information that I have, I talk to them, I show them things, they pay me money, the money goes into my PayPal account, I transfer the money from my PayPal account into my bank account into the United States. One hundred percent of my money is made online. How? I know things. I know things that other people don't know and they want to know them and I can explain these things to them very well. And then they're happy and they pay me money. I teach strange Internet things, I teach Adobe Illustrator, I teach Adobe Photoshop, I teach a language on the internet for web development called HTML, I teach another language called CSS, I teach search engine optimization, I teach how to create a WordPress page, using a specific theme called Divi, and I consult, I think I said in search engine optimization. Sometimes I'll do web development, but I would rather not. That's a whole different story and I just don't want to touch it actually. Also, I have approximately 70 books available on Amazon, which is great.

Every morning here in Guadalajara at 6.30 in the morning I take an hour of walk through a magnificent park and before I leave the apartment, the house, I check my Amazon stats to see how much money I've made up to 6.30 in the morning and then I check my stats an hour later when I get back to see how much money I made while I was in the park on Amazon. I also have a website with a subscription service, where people can watch my videos and see how to use Photoshop, how to make a website, blah-blah-blah-blah. That's a subscription, so people pay me like $6 a month, $11 a month, $20 a year, $37 a year, so through the day I get a subscription here, a subscription there, this is all just online money.

Now the question for you is what do you know that it's a little bit weird that people will pay you for just to talk to them and for you to solve problems that they have, that is important for them, that you can charge them $25 an hour and up. And many people, many normal people that are in industries, maybe it's healthcare, maybe it's law, maybe it's some type of social service, if you're a salesperson that sells something and you have an in-depth knowledge of this line of products....You have to think about it. What unique thing do you know that people would pay to talk to you about so that you can solve their problem and make money and then charge them a fee? Maybe you just want to charge them $15 an hour. You have to figure this out. And I don't know...On YouTube, Vimeo, on other video education websites, I mean you can go to YouTube and learn Photoshop. The problem with watching videos to learn things, because everybody that has a problem, that has a brain, the first thing they're going to do is go to Google and see if they can solve their problem for free on Google. Now, the problem with videos and Google is that you may get real close to solving your problem or learning about something, but you always have questions. And in watching a video, I watched many videos trying to learn something and I get through the whole video, like it's a 10-minute video, 15 minutes and then I get to the end and they didn't even talk about what I thought the video was going to talk about. It was a

15-minute waste of time. Or on videos that are educational I have questions about this, questions about this, questions about this. This is the beauty of you being with your client where they can ask questions live to their specific situation. Maybe it's money investment, maybe you know something about real estate. One of my clients is an immigration attorney who specializes in a special type of immigration. I mean, I have all kinds of really strange niche clients. So you have to think about what is it that you know that people want to know, that you can market and get people to call you on the phone, e-mail you and you can charge them to solve their problems. You know something, you just have to search for it.

In our next chapter we're going to go over helping people find you on the internet. And this is called Search engine optimization and it's not hard to do. You'll find this out in the next chapter. But for now, if you haven't gotten to this point and you would like to make this move and make money online working in your apartment, then you have to find that thing. Maybe it's a medical thing, maybe you're a nurse or something. If you're a psychologist, a psychologist that's dealing with, you know, or you just want to listen to people that are having this problem...I have a client who does horoscopes and she charges $90 an hour and she has a backlist of people that want to talk to her. It's all online.

But you have to give yourself some credit, think about what you know and think about how you can help other people with what you know. That's all it comes down to. It's there if you can just figure it out. Now the hesitation may be that many of my current clients...and I'm going to say every one of my clients that has e-mailed me for help initially or who has called me on the phone initially, after they explain their situation and how they need help and after I tell them how I can help them, well it comes to appointment time. And they say "Okay. What? Do I come to your place or do you come to my place?" And I'm going to say for five years I never told anybody I was in Mexico because sometimes they would freak out and many times they did freak out. But now I don't care because I'm making money, so they freak out, who cares? Okay? I've got a waiting list, okay? And some people are ready for the online experience, other people are not. But with the service that I use GoToMeeting. If you're talking about documents, you have legal documents, some kind of documents, maybe you want to teach web design, whatever, but in the GoToMeeting environment I can see my clients' computer live. When they're moving their mouse around, clicking on this and that, I see the movement live. If they want to show me this picture, that picture, this situation, I'm looking at it live. And then I can click a button and I can say "Well, look at my computer!" And then I can show them things live, images, how to do this, how to do that. I can show them everything live with FM quality sound. So with a new client, when it comes down to appointment time, I have to share with them how this works, just like I just told you. And they're always a little hesitant the first time, but five minutes into the first time is just like one-on-one. You have to get beyond the mindset that people have to be together in a room, looking at each other one-on-one to make things happen. You have to get beyond that mindset.

I know a woman here who is attempting to set up an international interpretation service Spanish to English, English to Spanish and she goes around to this place and this place and that place in her car in Guadalajara from place to place to place. That's a waste of time. She could do all of that on GoToMeeting. And I mean, it's going to be the same thing. Sure, you know, they can see her dress and her smile and all this personal touch, but when it all comes down to it, you're sharing information. And in my mind, 12 years down the road, if people aren't open to this experience, I don't want to deal with them anyway because, you know, like they're way behind the times, they are living like 100 years ago.

So you have to really move your mind beyond person to person. This is person to person. And when you're looking at somebody else's screen, they're looking at your screen, you're talking, all of the sudden you go into a very personal new world. It's very real and it works. And all of my customers in 12 years are amazed, they're just amazed at how powerful this whole situation is. So think about it. And you want to start looking for apartments in your city of choice in Mexico and see what the cost of living is going to be, how much are you seeing that you're going to have to pay out every month. So you want to put your model together, figure out how much money you're going to have to pay a month when you get to Mexico and then you want to launch your business while you're in the United States. And you want to test it and you want to see if you can surpass the amount of money that you need to pay for bills when you get to Mexico. And you want to test your system, so that it lasts for three months, where people are calling you on the phone, they're emailing you for your service, your clients are calling you for your service, you're making the money to pay enough to live in Mexico, you're making I'd say 20 to 25% more than what you need to live in Mexico or more you sustain this for three months solid, hopefully surprising yourself. And if you can sustain that for three months, then you're ready to move to Mexico, I would say without a problem. In our next chapter we're going to go into setting up your website and how to help people find you through search engine optimization.

Chapter 12 – Create Your Website. It's very easy.

In the last chapter I said in this chapter we are going to go right into search engine optimization, but then I was thinking, some of you may not have websites, so let's talk about getting your website set up. Setting up a website is very easy, but there are some steps that you really want to think about upfront that are very important.

The first thing you want to do is you want to get a URL. That is the name of your website. A URL would be something like huffingtonpost.com, cnn.com, abc.com, espn.com. Those are what you call URL's. They're kind of like license plates. And there are billions of websites, but none of the URL's can be duplicated. You can't have cnn.com, you can't have abc.com, you can't have fridays.com.

You have to come up with a unique URL. My suggestion is to come up with a very unique short URL. I had one client, her URL was like "my yoga shop in downtown Puerto Vallarta, my name is Sarah." Who can remember that and type it in to get to her website? So you want to come up with something maybe no more than twelve characters and something catchy, that kind of describes what your website is all about. Now, if you think about URL's like bestbuy.com, that tells you exactly. It's going to give you the best buys, but you might go weird with your URL. Think of walmart.com. What does "wal-mart" tell you about what they have in Wal-Mart? Wal-Mart has everything. Or sears.com. They don't tell you anything. So whatever it is, just think about it, brainstorm, and come up with a bunch of names. There is a website, you can just go to GoDaddy.com and they have a place there for check URL's or there's a website, it's called Whois.com, if I'm not mistaken. And if you go to Whois, that's W-H-O-I-S, Whois.com, then they have a little box and you can click in the little box that says "Find your domain name", search. And you type in whatever you made up and that will tell you if the domain name is taken or if it is available. Again, a domain name is like a license plate number and it is like a license plate also in that it has to be renewed every year. And the price for that is going to cost you somewhere between 8 to 12 dollars a year.

So brainstorm, come up with a URL name, then you need to find a web host. A web host is a company that has a bunch of computers and they host your website. It's almost like renting a garage. If you think of all your pictures and your words as a furniture where you put all of your furniture in this garage and leave it there and then you pay somebody to keep all your stuff. So a web host does the same thing, but instead of furniture they put your words and pictures there and make it accessible to the world, so that everybody can visit. So if I were you, I would get a reliable web host, the most reliable web host that I can think of are GoDaddy.com or Bluehost.com. I have about nine websites, all of my websites are hosted on Bluehost.com. I like Bluehost, they have 24/7, that means all the time technical support that you can call and talk to 24 hours a day, if you have any problems with your website. And their technical support is located in Utah, so all of the technical support people for Bluehost are Americans, they speak fluent English and the connection is very good and if you have MagicJack or Vonage in Mexico, you can call them and talk to them 24 hours a day about your website, and they will help you. So what you want to do is sign up with one of them, it's going to cost you 8 to 12 dollars a month. Both of those web hosts have a pricing so that if you pay them for 3 years at a time, it goes down to like $4 a month, if you want to make that investment. And Bluehost or GoDaddy, when you sign up with them, you can pay them for your annual URL fee, along with the regular monthly hosting fee. So there you go.

Now once you get signed up with Bluehost or GoDaddy, then you need the actual web page. Traditionally, and for years and years and years, web pages were hand coded. Hand coding means that you're going to have to write the HTML, CSS and PHP. I know how to do all three of those things.

And HTML is one language, CSS is another language and PHP is another language and they all have different syntaxes, meaning that it's like French has one syntax, English has another syntax and then Chinese has a totally different syntax. So to hand code a web page and sit down and I mean, sit down and write the code so that your pictures and your words and your header and your logo all show up in the right places, those are hand coded with code. Now, we're not going to do that. I'm not going to suggest you do that. I'm going to tell you how not to do that. But along with the hand coding, well in the past everybody was on the Internet with laptops and desktops, then the year 2013 was the year of responsive web design. Well, what does that mean? Responsive web design means that your website shows up appropriately on a small iPhone, on an iPad or other tablets, or larger than the iPhone, but smaller than an iPad is a Galaxy 7 Android. And then you have the laptop and then you have the desktop and yes, you have people surfing the Internet on big screen televisions. So you want your website to look appropriate with the images and the text on each of these devices. This is called developing a responsive website. Okay.

Now, if you're hand coding a site in your HTML and your CSS to get that done, you have to write a special code, so that when you make the screen small enough for an iPhone, it shows up okay there, but it shows up appropriately on a big screen television also. That's all hand coding. So a free software that does that for you, that is responsive is an application called WordPress. WordPress has come a long way. It does fabulous things. You can do WordPress and do no hand coding. All you have to do is type, click a button, put your pictures in, you don't have to know any code. The day of coding for people like you and for people like me is kind of like gone. We're at a point now where only corporations that make WordPress or maybe ESPN does some hand coding on their website, but those days are kind of gone. You can have a website now, maintain it and it's almost just like using Word.

So when you sign up for GoDaddy or for Bluehost, what you want to do is once you sign up you have your URL, they'll activate your URL. Once they activate the URL, you'll have a website. You can go to your URL, there'll be a blank page there. Now it's time to fill in the blanks. So once your URL is activated, what you want to do is call GoDaddy technical support or call Bluehost technical support and then what you want to have them do is install WordPress. Have them install WordPress! They can do that with a click of a button. I do this all the time for clients. I just call up one of them, "Bluehost, can you do a WordPress installation?" They say "yes", it might take about ten minutes because they have to connect it to a database, so you might have to wait. When they're done, you have WordPress and all you do is you go to your URL, let's say cnn.com and then you type "forward, slash, WP, dash, admin." That's universal. If you're ESPN, you go to espn.com, "forward, slash, WP, dash, admin" you type that, hit enter, and it takes you to your Log in. All you have to do is put in a user name and a password, click a button and you're into the situation where you can create pages, type text, add images, add forms, comments, links to other pages, all by just clicking buttons.

Now, the final step in WordPress is installing an appropriate WordPress theme. I don't want to go way into detail on this but themes run WordPress. It's like how your page is going to look. I have worked with thousands of clients and work with thousands of WordPress themes and for me, I'm telling all of my clients to use this theme and the theme is called Divi. It is responsive, it's very easy to use and I think it is the most versatile WordPress theme available. The great thing about Divi is it's being so popular internationally. If you want to know how to do anything, "Oh, I need a form over here on the left hand side, I need a full page, I need a full page screen, something that fills the screen, I need a video in the middle of my web page. How do I do this? How do I change my fund? How do I change my menu situation? Divi is so popular that you can get on the Internet and just type in Divi, change menu. Divi, add video. And you will see literally thousands of answers to your questions, so you're not left in the dark and you need to call your web developer.

Now on the other hand, you can pay someone

to build the website for you. I don't suggest this. Divi is easy enough to learn. And that way, if you wake up in the middle of the night and you want to change your website, you change your website. If you have a web developer, then you contact the web developer "Can you make this change? Can you make that change?" and you wait a couple of days and then you decide to change again all of a sudden. One small change that you wanted to make has taken you a week and in a week you've come up with like five other changes and you're constantly waiting for these changes to take place. If you learn how to use Divi, the theme within WordPress on your website, you are in total control, you can make changes on your own for free whenever you want.

You will want to use images on your website and in Google you can just go to Google and type in pictures of wheat fields, pictures of flowers, pictures of sunrises, pictures of the beach and there are literally thousands, if not millions of free non copyrighted images that you can get right off of Google and put into your website. You might want a logo. For image, I call it image manipulation. For a logo you might want something special. In that situation there is a website called Fiverr or F- I –V- E- R- R, fiverr.com. And on Fiverr there are thousands, tens of thousands of artists and translators, people do anything on Fiverr. And everybody on Fiverr charges $5 for everything, that's why they call it Fiverr. Now the thing about Fiverr is almost everybody that advertises on Fiverr is going to charge you more than $5. Some people will actually charge you $5 to do a basic logo. You get an account with Fiverr, you do a search in Fiverr for logo creation. There you will find a thousand people that will make a logo for $5. If you're going to do a logo, I would do a search for logos in Google and just look around at different logos and see one you like, find one that you like, save it, download it. All you have to do is right click on it and say "save image as", save it somewhere and then go to Fiverr, get an account with Fiverr, find a design artist you can work with and then you email them the logo that you like and you say "I want a logo that looks like this." And then you can have this person manipulate images for you, you can tell them that "I need this image for the top of my web page, I need this image for the side of my web page." If you really want to go all the way, you might want to invest in Photoshop. I'm a professional Photoshop user, I can make anything happen in Photoshop, but I think it's very handy on anybody that's going to have a web page to know how to take an image, add some text to the image and then make the width and height that will be appropriate for your web page. It's a business, it's an investment. Are you going to make or buy? Are you going to do it yourself or hire someone else to do it? So there you go. There is how you get your website set up, there is how you get a URL, there is how you get a web host, there is how you make your WordPress installation and then you install Divi as a theme to use in WordPress. Let me say that Divi will cost you $79 a year. You pay them $79, but it's extremely versatile. And I have videos on my website billthegeek.com/members that will show you how to use Divi and how you can control it to give it the look and feel that you want it to have. Okay. Now, in the next chapter we will go into Search Engine Optimization and how to help people find you on the Internet.

Chapter 13 – SEO, Search Engine Optimization. Helping People Find You.

No matter what consulting or service you have to offer, someone is looking for you right now, they're looking for you, they need help. So all you have to do is help them find you and they'll be very happy to work with you, they will want to give you money. Now personally, I don't need a million customers, I just need about 1000 people or even 100 or 200 people that want to work with me over a period of maybe a week to learn Photoshop. Maybe they want to learn some web development over the period of a week, maybe they want to learn how to do search engine optimization of the period of a couple of three hours. A couple of hundred people giving me like, you know, 500 to 1000 dollars a week, I'm good with that. I don't need a million people. A couple of hundred people, I'm good to go.

So with search engine optimization, the goal is

to help people find you, so that you have a steady stream of income, a steady stream of work. And almost every client that I've ever had, clients from five years ago call me up "Are you still doing this? I'm doing this. Can you help me with this situation that I'm in now?" They are your repeat customers. So let's talk about how search engine optimization can help you. Now what I'm going to ask you to do now is go to a computer and go to Google. And it's as simple as this. If you go to Google and you type in, and I'm doing this now as I write and talk for my audio tape, I'm going to go to Google and I'm going to type in "hotdogs" and I just hit enter and I get a bunch of websites for hotdogs. Now, as you look in Google at the very top of the screen, you can see where you typed in hotdogs, below the word hotdogs at about one inch...now as I do this, I'm on a desktop and it may show up a little bit different on a laptop and on a cell phone, I don't think the number that I'm going to talk about right now shows up at all. But on a laptop or a desktop if you look one inch below "hotdogs", you'll see a number, on my screen it says 83,000,000 results. That's your competition for hotdogs: eighty million. And for you to get on page one or two of Google for "hotdogs", that's pretty much impossible. Unless you're paying for ads. I don't pay for anything. What I'm looking at here, Wikipedia shows up number one. Okay. Now what your goal is to look at that and to come up with search terms for what you want to do for people. Now for me, I'm looking for clients in the United States. Pretty much all of my clients are in the United States, Canada, I have many clients in Great Britain, I have clients in Australia. Those countries have people with money that are willing to pay you on PayPal. So that's my market. I have an international English speaking market.

So what I'm trying to do, when I'm looking for Google search terms, I want to get this 80 million number down somewhere below a million. If I can find a keyword phrase, that's what we're talking about, this is a very important term, keyword phrase. Right now "hotdogs" is our keyword phrase. So we want to be able to talk in our keyword phrase and optimally that 80 million goes down to 500,000 or less. If I find a keyword phrase that shows up with that number that we're talking about at

500,000, I know I can get page one. 700,000, I can probably get on page one. You get up to a million, that's the shaky point. One million and over, it gets real shaky, real challenging, lots of competition. Okay, so I have hotdogs in there. Now, I'm going to type in hotdogs Chicago and I hit enter. Now, that 80 million number goes down to 6 million and the number may change on your machine, but now I'm at 6 million. That's way too high. It's better than 80 million, but it's way above 500,000 or 1,000,000. So now I'm going to type in "hotdogs Chicago Southside." Okay. Now I'm still getting 6 million and that's not quite...How about "best Chicago hotdog downtown?" I'm not getting numbers that I really like here, but let's try a real...something that works for me. I actually do teach Dreamweaver. Dreamweaver is a web development tool published by Adobe and you write your HTML, your CSS, your PHP, so I'm going to type in Dreamweaver teacher. Dreamweaver teacher. Okay. For Dreamweaver teacher, that number is at 681,000. And on my browser I see Dreamweaver teacher, Bill the Geek, you see Adobe at the very top, that is a paid add. But Dreamweaver teacher, Bill the Geek, that's me.

Internationally I'm number one for Dreamweaver teachers. I get calls from all over the world every week for Dreamweaver teacher. I make a lot of money and that's free advertising.

So that's what you want to do. You want to type in, you want to find a keyword phrase that is unique and first what you want to do is you want to sit down with a pen and paper and just write down a bunch of keyword phrases. And Google has changed. Keywords used to be words like hotdog. Okay? But now Google has expanded, so that people can type an entire sentence, perhaps you're consulting on immigration, so I'm going to type in immigration attorney. I'm just going to type in immigration attorney. Now that's at 8 million, but then I'm going to type in immigration attorney Columbus, Ohio. Okay, I typed that in. Now, immigration attorney Columbus Ohio brings the number down to 182,000. I can surely get on page one of Google with this keyword phrase.

Now as you come up with these ideas, you want to brainstorm. Maybe you would be happy with customers from throughout the United States, but you might pick a few cities and if you're a brain surgeon and you're going to consult on brain surgery from Mexico, okay, so you want to type in brain surgery Los Angeles. Brain surgery Des Moines Iowa. You want clients. So what you want to do is work with different key phrases and then attach a city with the State to it and that will bring the numbers down in Google. I mean if I was an immigration attorney with a website and I wanted to get some clients from Columbus Ohio, there you go. Right there. I can be page one with that. Okay.

So once you come up with a keyword phrase, then it's time to use the keyword phrase. Now how to use the keyword phrase? The next thing you want to do is go into WordPress, you have Bluehost, you have your URL, you've installed WordPress, you have Divi there. WordPress has access to these things called plugins. They're like little applications that help you do various things in your website. And there's a plugin for Search Engine Optimization. It's called Yoast, spelled like Toast, with a Y. You download the plugin, you install it and it helps you do your SEO. Google wants to see your keyword phrase used about five different ways in your website. First of all, at the very top of your website, if I am an immigration attorney in Columbus Ohio, I put that at the very top of my page and I make it a Heading 1 tag. Okay. That's a little HTML talk, but in WordPress you highlight the word and then...when you're in WordPress, it's just like being in Word. So you highlight the word, you click a button and you apply what is called a Heading 1 tag. It makes the text bold and black, and it's a header. Okay.

So now secondly, Google wants to see the keyword phrase five to six times in your document, in 300 words. So okay, I am an immigration attorney in Columbus Ohio and I would like to help you. Being an immigration attorney in Columbus Ohio, you will be very happy because I can help you because I'm an immigration attorney in Columbus Ohio. Now, it may sound kind of corny, but that's what Google wants. It wants a minimum of 300 words and it wants that keyword phrase to show up five to six times in those 300 words. Now what I'm going to tell you now is a little technical, but Yoast SEO shows you how to do what I'm about to tell you now. And also on my website, billthegeek.com/members I have videos on SEO. It's a link right on the top of the page, it says SEO, click on that and it will show you how to do this using Yoast SEO within Divi. What Google also wants is they want to see the keyword phrase in this thing called "meta description". In WordPress, in your little Yoast SEO box you click "meta description" and you paste your keyword phrase there. And then for your page, that's your meta description, and they want it in the title of your page, in the title tag of your page. When you create a page, there's a big blank rectangle at the very top of your WordPress page. It says "title." You want this keyword phrase as your title. That's pretty much it. You do that and you wait around for about a week. If you found a keyword phrase in Google where the competition is 500,000 or less, you wait about a week in Google and you should get to page one. Now the thing is in Google you never really know. Sometimes you can do your SEO perfectly and it doesn't show up. But generally speaking, this methodology does work and this is how I made all of my money for the last twelve years, using Search Engine Optimization. Now watch my videos at billthegeek.com/members, click the SEO button, I'll show you exactly how to do your SEO. And let me say this. Each page of your website is a different marketing universe. One page, you may be saying immigration attorney Columbus Ohio. You will or can have a totally different page, that is immigration attorney Atlanta Georgia, immigration attorney Jacksonville Florida. Each page is its own marketing tool. So in the immigration attorney Jacksonville Florida page for the title of the page it would be immigration attorney Jacksonville Florida. You would have 300 words, using that keyword phrase five to six times, you would have at the top of the page or your header, where you select the text and apply the heading tag to the text, your meta description, all of that it would change from page to page to page.

So now I teach Photoshop, I teach Dreamweaver, I teach SEO, and each of those pages is a different mechanism for Google, so that people will call me on the phone and I can help them. I'm helping people find me through Google and then I work with them and they pay me through PayPal. Now, once you get this set up, then you want to open a Google Analytics account. That's free. You go to Google and type in Google Analytics. You'll see at the top of the page, it'll say Google Analytics, you click that and then what you do is you set up a Google Analytics account. It's very easy. The benefits of a Google Analytics account is that you can go to Google every day and see how many people are visiting your website, you can see what countries these people are coming from and not only does it tell you how many people are visiting your website, but it will show you on a daily basis how many hits you are getting on each and every page. Maybe you're getting a lot of hits on the Atlanta Georgia page, but you're not getting any hits on the Boise Idaho page. So then you make changes to see how you can get more hits on all of your pages. This is very beneficial and you can see if your SEO is working at all. Maybe you're getting zero hits. But you do want to open a Google Analytics account and what happens is Google

Analytics is going to give you a number that identifies all of the pages on your web page under one umbrella. So it's almost like a social security number for your website through Google and what you will do is you will copy this social security number, your Google Analytics ID number, and there's a little place in WordPress where you paste that number in into Yoast SEO, and then all of your pages can be tracked by Google Analytics. You have to have Google Analytics and you need to check your Google Analytics every day. It can be very rewarding, it can be very frustrating if you're getting zero hits. But if your SEO is working and you can see that you're getting like twenty hits a day on this page, thirty hits a day on that page, sixty hits a day on this page, it's very rewarding to see that your marketing is working.

Now everybody knows what Facebook is, but very few people know what Google Plus is. Google Plus is Google's Facebook. But not very many people use it. But for every page on your website... Well, first of all you want to open a Google Plus account. Then you have a Google Plus page, which is like Facebook, and you can write articles and put pictures on there. The only thing I use Google Plus for is every time I create a new page on my website I open Google Plus, I copy the URL of the new web page and I post it in Google Plus. It gives you Google brownie points and it ups your rankings in the Google search engine. Because they like it that you're using not Facebook, but Google Plus.

So that's a short version of SEO. I'm going to blow my horn, I do consult on SEO. If you want to call me at 415 839 0096, that's 415 839 0096, I'll be happy to give you an hour consultation. And if you have your WordPress site all set up, you've installed your Yoast SEO plugin, you have Divi installed, in an hour I can show you exactly what to do. And most likely you'll be ready in an hour if you take notes and then maybe a week later you might want to do a half an hour session with me. That is search engine optimization and you want to test, you want to get...Before you come to Mexico, if you don't already have an online business that's bringing in the money, then you want to get your website set up, get your SEO working and you want to test this for three months to see if your phone is ringing and if you are getting clients. If your phone's not ringing, if people aren't emailing you, then it's not working and you don't want to be in Mexico with a hopeful online business. Okay? So that is a bit of a summary of Search Engine Optimization, helping people find you through Google.

Chapter 14 – Immigration, Visas and other stuff

It's a really good thing to be legal down in Mexico. It's just a nice thing because if you're down here and they find out that you're illegal, what they do is they just either put you on a plane and send you back to the United States or they put you on a bus and send you back to the United States or wherever you're from, you have to leave. So being legal is a good thing. Now whether you fly into Mexico or take a bus into Mexico, you automatically when you cross the border get a 180-day visa. That costs about $25-26. If you're flying into Mexico, that's added into your airfare, so you really don't even know it. You'll be on the plane about a half an hour away from Mexico, the flight attendant will give you some paperwork that you have to fill out like "do you have any live animals with you or fruits or how much money do you have with you in cash?" You're not allowed to bring…Or they want to know if you're bringing in more than 10,000 dollars. But anyway, you know it's no big deal, you sign the papers, filling out, putting your name, your passport number and you're good to go.

Another thing is you do need a passport to get into Mexico. And when your plane lands, they will check your passport and they'll check all of your luggage to see if you have any goodies in there that you shouldn't have. And that's about it. And then I know many people that have lived here for like fifteen years, they don't have anything beyond a 180-day visa. So what they'll do is they'll fly on day like 179, they'll fly back into the United States, maybe visit some people, buy some stuff at the grocery store that's not readily available in Mexico, like Miracle Whip…I'm dying for some Miracle Whip. I haven't had any Miracle Whip in like five years. I grew up on Miracle Whip. So people will fly back to the United States, say hello to friends and family, then come back, then they're good for another six months. And I use that methodology for about four years, but the thing is it's kind of bit expensive like to fly to Houston or to fly to San Antonio, I mean that's going to cost you $300-400, you get lazy and you say "Oh, never mind". So all of a sudden you slip in…you're like a month illegal. So what do you do? Well, what happens is in Mexico you can pay for about anything. I mean that's something to keep in mind also about Mexico. It's very flexible. If you want to get something done, you show some people some money and it gets done.

So two times I was illegal. And one time I was quite fortunate. In fact, I think this happened to me four times. Two times I went to the airport and well, first I had a landlord, his name was Don, a great person. He owns Casa Cupula Resort in Puerto Vallarta. And I knew I overstayed, I knew he had a lot of experience with clients who had overstayed also. I said "Don, what do I do, what do I do? I have to leave the country. How am I going to get out of here?" Because if you're illegal, they might not let you out of the country, then you're just stuck at the border, if you're trying to figure out how to get out of the country. So Don told me "Go to the airport and lie." Okay? And that's what I did. I went to the airport and I told them that I lost my 180-day visa. Now your 180-day visa is just a piece of paper, okay? And I've never carried it around with me. We'll get to that in a moment. But I told them that I was at the beach and it got all wet and then it floated away into the ocean and so this guy took me to some other guy and I gave this guy 300 pesos, he gave me some piece of paper and then when I went back to the ticket counter, which is where you need your visa to get out of the country, he gave me a piece of paper to give to the ticket counter lady and then I was out of the country. I lied like that two times. The third time wasn't so easy. The third time I was flying out of Mexico City, from Puerto Vallarta to Mexico City, and the lie didn't work. These people wanted some verification like when I got into the country, some proof when I got into the country. Now fortunately, my father had visited me like a couple of months before I was at this airport trying to get out and fortunately, his name is the same as my name William D. Louis. Even though I'm William D. Louis Jr, it just so happened that I had a copy of his flight itinerary in my laptop. So out of desperation, because I really wanted to catch my connecting flight to the United States and get out of Mexico, I opened up my laptop, I showed them this flight itinerary, it even had a copy of the ticket in there, they went for it and I was able to catch my flight. Tell you what, that's just nerve-racking. All of those situations are nerve-racking.

After I went through that, when I came back to Mexico, I got an immigration attorney. And I just got on the internet and did a search for immigration attorneys, Puerto Vallarta. And I found a wonderful female immigration attorney, Elizabeth Guzman, Puerto Vallarta, Mexico. She has a website and she helps people buy and sell real estate, very competent, a bilingual. So she took me through the documentation to get a one-year visa and that was pretty cool. A one-year visa, you're legal for one year. After six months you don't have to fly in, fly out, that's a big hassle, that's like $400 to $600 that you save or the time of getting on a bus and taking ten hours to get to the border, ten hours to get back. It's just like very relaxing. They give you a little card, it looks like a driver's license. Okay. Now, to get that one-year visa, all the visas as far as applications go and applying are kind of the same. There are immigration offices, I've dealt with the immigration offices in Puerto Vallarta and in Guadalajara. In Puerto Vallarta what they wanted was a copy of my passport, I had to give them fingerprints and they wanted, I forget whether it was, I think it was three months of bank statements. They want to make sure that you have a source of income or money in the bank. Now my attorney Elizabeth right upfront, I said "Well, how much money do they want me to have in the bank?" She told me 10,000 dollars. In my case, I was cool with that. But I think if you have some bank statements and just show that you have some income, I don't think that you're going to need 10,000 dollars. I think they just want to see that you have like 1000 dollars in the bank and in your bank statement, if they see some deposits in there. That's what I think. Okay.

So you fill out these papers, she filled out the papers for me, then she went down to Immigration with me. The most difficult thing for me in immigration was my signature. I have a wild crazy signature and I can't duplicate my signature more than one time. So I feared this point when it's all said and done and they've approved all your paperwork, you have to do the signature. And two times I have had to do my signature at their little front desk like 50 to 80 times until I had one that looks like what my passport looks like. Next time I get a passport which comes up for renewal in three years, I'm going to create a signature that is very easy to duplicate. I tell you that. That's one thing to look out for. But anyway, that's the one-year visa.

Now, there's a two-year visa. Currently I have a two-year visa, I'm getting ready to renew my third two-year visa. I'm going to say about two years ago they changed immigration policy, so that you could go from a one-year to a permanent visa. I would prefer a permanent visa. Then I don't have to deal with going to Immigration at all forever. But the catch in my situation is I have a car, a Lexus that was made in Japan. I don't know if they make Lexus's alike in the United States, I'm sure they do somewhere, but my identification number on my dashboard indicates that my particular Lexus was made in Japan. And you cannot nationalize a car in Mexico that was actually manufactured in Japan. What the heck? So I can't sell my car down here, but with a two-year visa your car is associated with your visa and you don't have to get Mexican license plates. So I've had the same license plate for about six years from Ohio. Okay? Which is a good thing. I don't have to worry about that. But in your situation, you come down here, get your 180-day visa, find an immigration attorney, there are many of them readily available and that's all they do. And because of the business they are in they are bilingual. And they'll talk to you just like a normal person and say "Well, we'll need this, this and that." I think I paid Elizabeth, the first time I think I paid her like 4000 pesos, for the two-year visa I think I paid her like 5000 pesos. And then there's a fee that you have to pay the government for the visa. I think that comes to about 450 pesos. Now, if you're driving into

Mexico with your car, you want to have all of your documentation for your car, you want to have your title. If your car is not paid for, you want to have all of the documentation because they are going to check that at the border and then you're going to have to buy some kind of sticker to stick in your windshield, so that you're legal to have your car in Mexico. That's going to cost you about $250 at the border, which is refundable after some period of time. I think it's like after a 180 days. So there's your 180-day visa, that's only $25 to $26. There's your 1-year visa. You can get a 2-year visa or a permanent visa, but be legal.

I had an associate and he was just too wild and crazy and he got drunk and went on a series of taxi rides in Puerto Vallarta with the same taxi driver. I mean, he went here, there, here, there, here, there and he didn't have any money to pay the taxi driver, so the taxi driver called the police. The police actually just took him to prison. So they took him to prison, he didn't have any money to get out. Mexican prisons...I've never been in one, I've never visited one, but in my imagination if you can think of

American prisons, just prison is a no-no. Okay? But anyway, he's in a Mexican prison and he didn't have any money to get out. So finally, a judge decided to let him out. So when he's leaving the prison, he was illegal. He hadn't renewed his visa, so they let him out of prison, but when he walked out of the prison door, the immigration people were there and they deported him to Arizona. So just be legal! Be legal, feel good, be happy!

Chapter 15 – Getting Healthcare

Healthcare in Mexico is very good. The doctors are very good, the hospitals are very clean, you know, some of these hospitals are nicer than in the United States. In Puerto Vallarta I was shocked at the equipment that they had, how professional the doctors were, the cleanliness of the environment, it was really wonderful. Healthcare in Mexico is about, I'm going to say at least 50% less as what it's going to cost in the United States. The cost will shock you. When I talked about the dentist in another chapter, to get your teeth cleaned is only going to cost you $25 to $30, to get a cap on your tooth is only going to cost you maybe $150 to $200. When the dentist drills here and drills there, it's only going to be a fraction of what it costs in the United States. To visit a doctor and pay for a doctor's visit, so he can take a blood test, do an evaluation, that's only going to cost you about $25 to $30. Doctors in Mexico don't make big money. I went to my girlfriend's family, she has nine brothers and sisters and a mother and they all go to the same doctor's office. Now, this doctor's office is not as modern as the hospitals are, it's very clean, but it's like a doctor's office you might go to like seventy years ago. But the guy knows what he's doing and her whole family goes there. And this is a doctor's office, but it kind of works like a hospital also. So if you get really sick and you need to spend the night, they have rooms with beds and a television, just like a regular hospital, but it's not as modern. It's like going back seventy years as far as what the accommodations look like. But this doctor, I had a problem with my foot and so he had another doctor that works in his little complex, that is a foot doctor, and this doctor gave me like an hour and a half of his time, he took a look at my foot, it wasn't really a bad problem and he did all these things to it. It took him like an hour and a half. And I was leaving and I said "Well, how much do I owe you?" And he said "Oh, 200 pesos." Two hundred pesos is like 10 dollars. He gave me an hour and a half of his time, I mean okay, and he did a very good job. I haven't had a problem since.

Now I had a problem...I'm getting kind of personal here, but I had a problem with a cyst on my butt. Okay? And at the time I was headed to Puerto Vallarta and I had scheduled surgery to remove it here in Guadalajara, but my girlfriend's daughter's boyfriend is a doctor in Guadalajara. He says "Oh, when you're on vacation down here, just give me a call and we'll set an appointment at the public hospital." So I got an appointment at the public hospital, it was free. Now the public hospital is different than the private hospitals. We'll talk about this in a minute, because the public hospitals that's where everybody can go and it's kind of free.

We'll talk about that in a second. So this situation is totally unorganized and if my girlfriend wasn't there with me to walk me through the process and if her daughter's boyfriend hadn't hooked us up with a specific doctor and if I had been there by myself, I think I would have been totally lost and probably would have spent hours, just trying to figure out, hours in finding and hours in waiting. This is what happens at a public hospital if you don't speak Spanish. I suggest you getting some form of health insurance. You never know. In the United States, when you're walking down the sidewalk, let's say you have a sidewalk and at the edge of the sidewalk there's like a 40 foot drop. Well, in the United States they have laws that you're going to have to have some form of protection, so that if people walk off of this 40 foot drop, well in the United States if you don't have a fence or something there, then the people that fall off they're going to sue you and take everything you have. They don't have laws like that in Mexico. If you have a sidewalk, it may be beautiful, but there's no fence, no curb, it's just a 40 foot drop off, then you walk off there near this SOL (shit out of luck)…and there's all kinds of designs down here that are totally dangerous. They're very pretty, but it's very dangerous and the sidewalks and the streets have holes and things that a body can fit through. And if you're not watching where you're walking, it's very easy to break a hip, break an arm, break a leg, so you never know when you're going to end up in the hospital.

So you can buy insurance. I didn't buy insurance and so I had been here like eleven years and a friend of mine who wasn't quite the most responsible individual ended up breaking both his arms and a leg and ended up in the public hospital. And he had no money. The hospital wouldn't do anything for him until somebody came up with a large sum of money to take care of him. They kept him at the hospital, but he had a bed in the hallway in the public hospital. He was in there for like a month before friends of his raised money and then they shipped him to Florida, okay? I don't really even know what happened to him. But after I saw that happen to him, my girlfriend's sister-in-law sells insurance. And I told her this story and I told her that I wanted a health insurance and she fixed me up, so that now I have very excellent health insurance, I have a high deductible because it's only for emergencies. The deductible is like $500. Okay. Fine. This is my second year with this health insurance policy. I've never had to use it, okay? So I pay approximately $1300 a year for this insurance and it gets me into the best hospitals in Mexico, none of that public, chaotic stuff. You get into the best hospitals in Mexico where the rich people go. Okay. I'm not proud, I want to go where the rich people go, where the good doctors are, where you have wonderful clean rooms with good food and cable television. Okay? That's where I want to go if I break my arm or my leg. Now you can get or you can sign up for the government's free public health program. It doesn't cost you any money. I do believe that you need a one-year, two-year or a permanent visa to obtain this. This is what my girlfriend has, she has public Mexican insurance and she just renewed hers and she talked to them about me. She says "Well, can my boyfriend get this insurance with his visa?" And they said yes. Talk to your friends, once you get to Mexico talk to other Canadians, talk to Americans, talk to them about their health insurance. I know that in Mexico there's an organization, you can Google them on the Internet, it's called Expats in Puerto Vallarta. They have a newsletter. And they have a few people that advertise on their newsletter on how to obtain healthcare insurance. So it's almost like maintaining your visa status. Something goes wrong and something goes wrong and bad things happen. And the same with healthcare. Who knows what might happen and when? So get yourself be legal with your visa and get yourself hooked up with some health insurance, so if something goes wrong, you can still be happy.

Chapter 16 – Getting Auto Insurance and a Mexican Driver's License

Getting auto insurance down here is really no problem and it's extremely reasonable in price. When I was living in one apartment all of a sudden I ended up with a car and I needed automobile insurance and the landlord had an automobile insurance agent. His name was Paco and I've been buying my automobile insurance from Paco for about six years now. It started out costing about $250 a year. I paid my premium about two months ago and it has gone up over six years. Now it's about $430 a year. The law says down here that you have to have automobile insurance if you have a car and you need to keep the documentation in your car with you all of the time. So it's not a problem. Again talk to your fellow expats, see who's driving a car and ask who is their automobile insurance agent. Now, the last driver's license...I had a California driver's license for five years, then I moved back to Ohio, got an Ohio driver's license and then when I brought the car back to Mexico, the Ohio driver's license expired and I needed to get a Mexican driver's license or some type of driver's license. If you have a United States driver's license, that's all you need until it expires. So if you have a car, a driver's license from the United States, you're okay until it expires, but then you need some type of license to drive your car.

So I was living in Puerto Vallarta and I went to

my immigration attorney, Elizabeth, I said "Elizabeth, I need a driver's license." And Puerto Vallarta is in the state of Jalisco. Jalisco, Puerto Vallarta. Jalisco. Okay, so I was going to have to take a driver's license exam to get a Mexican driver's license which I was very uncomfortable with because that was going to be in Spanish. Okay? So Elizabeth said "Okay, I'll get you all set up. Just be here tomorrow at 10 o'clock in the morning." So I said okay. So I go down there at 10 o'clock in the morning and there's some guy she introduces me to and I get in his car. She didn't go. I get in his car, then we go to some other guy's house and some community somewhere and we wait for this guy for like 20 minutes, this other guy I don't know, waiting on this guy who's like late, we're just sitting in the car waiting for the guy, so finally the guy comes out, they know each other, they're talking, they're happy and then they have another guy who's a friend of this other guy...So I'm in the car with these three guys that I don't know and so we get in the car and we drive for about a half an hour. We drive to another state in Mexico called Nayarit, which is apparently 30 minutes from Puerto Vallarta, not in the state of Jalisco, but in the state of Nayarit. Okay? So we go right to this Department of Motor Vehicles in Nayarit and there are people in there taking exams at the computers, a big line of people. And with my guy, only one of these guys goes in there with me. And of course, you have to have your passport and that's about it. All you need is a passport, so I walk in with my passport, we go to the front of the line, the guy behind the counter knows the guy that I am with and he says "Oh, okay" and some paperwork goes down and I sign, all I do is I put in a signature. And then the guy says "Okay." Then they take me over to this computer where this lady takes the paperwork, type some stuff in the computer, hits a button and out comes my laminated driver's license with my picture on it. Okay. Then we leave. So you know, the whole bit was like two hours, but my time in the Department of Motor Vehicles was about ten minutes. I was in and out, in ten minutes I went right to the front of the line and in front of the other people staying in the line. It was all about payola.

Now when I moved to Guadalajara, then I

needed a driver's license because I had a change of address so I had to get a driver's license. Presently, I don't have an immigration attorney in Guadalajara, so I had to go through the whole thing of getting a driver's license, like by myself. Fortunately, my girlfriend is Mexican, she speaks Spanish and she went to the Department of Motor Vehicles with me. So to get a driver's license from scratch I needed a passport, I needed my visa, a copy of my visa and I needed some form of utility bill. A utility bill can be from the electric company, from the water company, from a cable company, a phone bill. So I had to take a printed copy of my most recent Izzi cable bill. So we get there and there's a lot of people, hundreds of people in line and it went fairly smoothly. And the people locally, that's only like a half of mile away, they said I wouldn't have to take an exam and I was relieved that I wouldn't have to take an exam, but this was my first Mexican driver's license, so surprisingly when I got there I had to take an exam. And when they told me I had to take an exam, my panic level went to like grade 91. So they said okay, so they were making me wait so that I could take the exam on a computer and I asked them "So what are we waiting for?" because there were some empty computers and they said "we're waiting for our translator to show up so that he can help you understand the questions on the computer." And I thought wow. Right? So we go to the computer and the Mexican driver's license exam on the computer consists of ten questions and the questions are all with pictures. It's almost like a cartoon, okay? It's unbelievably simple. I had to take a driver's license exam in Ohio. I actually studied, that was like thirty questions. And you can only miss like, you know, three or some kind of weird thing like that. So with the ten questions they ask you, you can only miss two. So there are questions like they show a picture of a road in the country and some cows in the middle of the street. I swear to God. And so the question is: If you see this, what do you do? And two answers: go, run over the cows or stop. Okay. And then the questions are in Spanish, so I look at the guy and I say "Okay, so what's the question?" He says "So what do you do, go or stop?" And then I think one or two of the questions are kind of on the edge of, you know how those questions are, they're on the edge of well, I'm not really sure what do you do in this situation. Okay? I think I missed one of the questions, but the exam was very easy, very common sense ten questions. And I was out of there with my brand new Mexican driver's license. So it was really not difficult at all and I most likely could have gotten in and out of there without any help from my Spanish speaking girlfriend. So it was very simple and the whole process only cost I think like right around 20 dollars to get that thing in my pocket. And once you get it one time, then the next time you go back to renew it. You don't have to take an exam, you just have maybe your passport with you, your visa, showing your papers and they just right there on the spot print out anew just like in the United States. So there's your information on getting auto insurance and your Mexican driver's license and I believe you can use your Mexican driver's license in the United States as well.

Chapter 17 – Buying a House in Mexico

As an American or a Canadian you can own a

home in Mexico and the homes are very affordable. If you live in California or New York you'll get shocked with the type of values you can get for a home down here for maybe a hundred and fifty, a hundred thousand, a hundred and twenty thousand, a hundred and fifty thousand. It's a little different down here as far as how you pay for your homes. Most Mexicans will just pay cash for a house. Cash is huge down here. You can get financing through a Mexican bank, but the interest rates are very high. And then you have to verify that you have some source of income or some type of money in the bank to finance it. The interest rates are way more than in the United States, so cash is the way to go down here. But you can buy a house. Now what my last landlord did in Puerto Vallarta, he had some cash and he bought a house for like $80,000 and it was dilapidated, so he decided he was going to make this thing like a Marriott hotel, which he did. It took him about a year to do it and it's beautiful...I mean it's unbelievable. It does look like a Marriott hotel all the way through. And you can do that with marble floors, beautiful woodwork and the prices for the materials and the workmanship is excellent.

But fortunately, my landlord, he's gay, he has a partner and his partner knows everything about anything, about plumbing, electricity, drywall, which they don't use in Mexico. Everything is brick and mortar, which is wonderful. All the houses have total solid foundations and you can be in one room and make a bunch of noise and nobody's going to hear you because everything is built so tight. But anyway, fortunately for Mike and Charlie, Charlie was the know-it-all. Charlie knew about electricity and they wanted well-grounded electricity, so he had to direct the electricians on how to get that done. Now, when it comes to buying a house and renovating it, there are people that will offer their services to you and they have no clue what they're doing. And some of them will have documents that will say that they are a certified electrician, yet it will be a false document and they are preying on the ignorance of Canadians and Americans. Mike and Charlie told me that during the construction numerous times they had electrical boxes sitting around the house, a bunch of marble that was getting ready to be installed for flooring and the next day they would show up and it was all gone. It was almost like an inside job and then they were being overcharged. And they were both innocent, they were new to Mexico and they didn't know anybody in Mexico, so they were doing this for the first time, thinking that people were honest and straightforward and they ended up paying like double, instead of maybe an additional 200,000 they ended up paying an additional 400,000 to get everything done.

So if you're going to buy a house, first of all get a real estate, get a Mexican real estate attorney. There are all types of real estate offices in Mexico and there are many Americans and Canadians that are in this business. They are Mexican real estate brokers. So you want to contact these people and ask them for a list of reputable plumbers and electricians and only work with those people. It will save you a lot of time, save you a lot of money. The real estate environment as far as real estate sales goes is different than in the United States. In the United States you have brokers and they're all in this vast computer system and when a house goes up for sale, every broker in the city knows that this house goes up for sale and they all compete with their salespeople to sell this house. Well, they don't have...I think it's called a multi-listing system in Mexico, so Mexican real estate brokers, they know houses for sale and they don't tell anybody else about it. That's just within this group of brokers, that's it's kind of like a club. I know in Puerto Vallarta, they have like six brokerage groups and they kind of hide information on what's for sale, what's been sold, what's coming up for sale, so it's a totally different environment. But I know many Americans in Puerto Vallarta that own homes and the homes were very inexpensive, they've done some marvelous renovations. Where I was living in Puerto Vallarta a Canadian couple bought a house across the street from where I was living. And right after they purchased the house some very impoverished Mexicans moved in, it was like two couples, the men were brothers, both of the families had like three kids and they found the place was empty after it was sold and they just moved all their stuff in there and the Canadians can't get them out and the law in Mexico kind of sort it is, well, if people are in there you can't get rid of them. And they've been in there for like four years and the Canadian couples have been trying to get them out for four years and they can't get them out. I don't think the Canadian couple lives in Mexico. They were buying it as an investment property so that they could fix it up and move in one day, but these other people have been living in there, I don't know if you want to call it legal, illegal, but they can't get the people out. They have a type of real estate insurance. When you buy a house it costs about $300 extra on top of the house and if something like that happens, some people move in, they don't want to leave, you know, they're not paying rent living there, well, this $300 means that should this happen to you, the police come and they forcibly move these people out. Having said that, the Airbnb is down here. And if you go to look Guadalajara and if you go to Google and search for Guadalajara Airbnb, there are many Bed and Breakfasts in Puerto Vallarta owned by Canadians and Americans and that's another business. If you can rent an entire house and turn it into an Airbnb house or if you have the cash to buy a house and turn it into an Airbnb house, it's a very lucrative business I know in Puerto Vallarta and in Guadalajara. But the thing is I kind of think you're going to have to live there and monitor everything, but that's just another option. So for those of you that are interested in owning a home, I know right now my girlfriend is selling her house. It's a beautiful house in a wonderful neighborhood in Guadalajara, one of the best neighborhoods that exist in Guadalajara. It's like a four bedroom, four bathroom, front yard, back yard, Oxxo on the corner, pharmacy on the corner, luxurious grocery store two blocks away, Little Caesars pizza on the corner, the gas station is on the corner, but the house is a half a block away from the main street, it's very quiet, lots of trees, about two blocks away from one of the most fabulous parks, giant fabulous parks with all kinds of trees and yoga classes in the daytime and early morning. But she's selling the house for like five million pesos, which comes out to like $200,000. Yes, you can own a home in Guadalajara or Mexico, if that's what you're into.

Chapter 18 – Romantic relationships in Mexico

Well, you get down here, you had your apartment all set up, you're doing your job, doing your business, putting that money into your United States bank account, you've got your visa, maybe you have some health insurance, all is good.

Mexico is a beautiful place with many different things to do, you might get the...you fall in love. So bring that on with great precaution. If you're an American or Canadian and you want to stick with American and Canadian well, that's a wonderful thing being with someone that speaks English. Hopefully, they have some source of income. Mexico is notorious for Americans and Canadians that have just disappeared into Mexico and these are some of the people you may be meeting. Most people on the up and up, just straight up and up good people, but I am aware of some situations where women with money have fallen in love with an American or Canadian that they thought was a good person and they marry him and the next thing they know this person is gone and their bank account is empty. So just use all of the precautions that you would use in the United States.

If you decide to fall in love with a Mexican, use the same precautions. Mexico is a very family oriented country. I know that some families are very family oriented in the United States and Canada also, but multiply that times a hundred down here, because many families down here have...You meet somebody, they have like nine brothers and sisters and a mother and then nine aunts and uncles and then on one side of the family nine aunts and they get together every weekend and they're together all the time and people come into your house all the time.

I mean you'll see 16-year-olds walk around with like three kids. It seems like, you know, let's have babies without a job, okay? And then you have the 16-year-old who have three kids and live with their mom with like her two sisters, they each have two kids. And I remember I was doing some internet dating and I was pretty much interviewing this prospect over the phone and I said well, how many kids do you have? Well, I have three kids. So where do you live? I live with my mother. So do you have a job? No. Okay. So I want to date you. You have three kids, you live with your mom, you have no job. Okay? I mean this is after many years in Mexico of screening and I was getting my pants altered with a tailor and he and a friend were in there and he asked me "So what kind of woman are you looking for?" And we were joking around, we were having a good time. I said well, I'm looking for a Mexican woman who both her parents are dead, she has no brothers or sisters and she has a job. Okay? And they both just started laughing and the tailor, he said oh, Google that. Okay. Google that.

So be very cautious, male or female. Screen your applicants like "do you have a job?" That's the main thing. Do you have a job? And if I spend time with you and if I get close to you and you know maybe we live together does that mean your family's going to be living in our house? I mean do you have like ten kids that are going to be all of the sudden Junior and Sally and Maria are going to be living in our house with like five kids. I mean, you know, really beware. Screen, screen, screen. Puerto Vallarta is different because that environment is all about hotels and tourism. So a vast majority of Mexicans are working, cleaning hotel rooms, or waiters, waitresses, you know, and not making hardly any money. So the opportunity to hook up with a Canadian or American with any kind of income is like a Cinderella story. Guadalajara is filled with professional single Mexicans with real money. You come to Guadalajara, you're going to see all types of BMW's, AUDI's, Mercedes, and lots of brand new cars, single women and men that own their houses that are very nice. In Puerto Vallarta you might see one Mercedes in like three years. A BMW, if you see a BMW, that's odd. But Guadalajara is very sophisticated.

I would suppose the same is true to Mexico City. And I'm not saying that money will bring you happiness, but I know that in my life I don't want to be in a situation where I'm just paying out a lot of money with somebody that has no interest in life other than having babies and drinking beers and just sitting around and watching TV and figure out how much more money they can get out of my bank account. So ha-ha-ha. Having said that, it's a beautiful country with beautiful people, wonderful things to do, but be on the lookout when it comes for that time when you're looking at the sunset and you don't have anybody and you're looking for love. Beware and be lucky and be happy.

Chapter 19 – The Summary

Well, I hope I provided you with a bit of information that can help you actually come down here and I hope that I have shared with you some actual facts as far as how to make the move, how to be safe with your move, how to be legal with your move, how to be healthy with your move and how to be happy with your move. One thing that I really want to add in the summary is Mexico is so beautiful. And you may move to a beach location and there's so much to do, so many bars, so many parties, you can party all day. But if you're launching this online business, stay in your apartment, work hard. Work hard, work hard, focus. There are a lot of retirees from Canada and the United States with nothing to do. They have nothing to do, but do nothing. And they want to do nothing with you. And it happened with some Mexicans also, people with nothing to do and they want to do nothing with you. Avoid these people. Do your business, find other people that are doing business, people that have things to do, healthy people that like to work out, that like to think, that like to read, maybe they're close to your business, maybe they can help your business, but for a while until you get your business up and running so that the money is coming into the bank account and you're feeling comfortable and confident with your business just stay at home, work a lot, maybe go out in the morning for a beautiful walk, in the evening perhaps go out and get some taco stands, but work hard, focus on your website, focus on your online business and everything will go very well. Again, this is Bill the Geek. Visit my website at www.billthegeek.com/members,

I have videos on there on how to create your

Divi website as well as tutorials on search engine optimization. I do one-on-one private counseling, using GoToMeeting. You can see my screen, my computer screen, I can see your computer screen. We have FM quality sound. As of this date in 2017 I charge $45 an hour, you pay me after the session via PayPal. We can do a half an hour session, an hour session, an hour and a half session, two-hour session. I have all of these PayPal buttons on my website, so when you leave our session you pay the appropriate amount. If you don't learn anything, you don't pay. That's why you pay at the end of the session. It's been my pleasure. Visit my website. If you have any questions, comments, drop me an email or a comment from the website and hopefully I will respond promptly. Again, this is Bill the Geek signing off and I hope you come down and live a prosperous abundant and happy life in Mexico.

Made in the USA
Lexington, KY
27 November 2017